COUNTING *and* CONTEMPLATING BLESSINGS *and* ARCHETYPES *on* MATTHEW'S MOUNTAINS

Using The Rule *of* Nines

Counting and Contemplating Blessings and Archetypes on Matthew's Mountains

Copyright © 2025 Richard G. Manning M.D.. All rights reserved.

No rights claimed for public domain material, all rights reserved. No parts of this publication may be reproduced, stored in any retrieval system, or transmitted in any form or by any means, electronic, mechanical, recording, or otherwise, without the prior written permission of the author. Violations may be subject to civil or criminal penalties.

ISBN: 978-1-63308-764-4 (paperback)
        978-1-63308-765-1 (ebook)

Cover and Interior Design by *R'tor John D. Maghuyop*

PO Box 1665, Rolla MO 65402

Printed in United States of America

COUNTING *and* CONTEMPLATING BLESSINGS *and* ARCHETYPES *on* MATTHEW'S MOUNTAINS

Using The Rule *of* Nines

RICHARD G. MANNING M.D.

TABLE OF CONTENTS

Dedication 7
Prologue: Counting the Nine Blessings 9
Chapter 1:   Contemplating the Sixth 11
Chapter 2:   Contemplating the Third 19
Chapter 3:   Contemplating the Fourth 27
Chapter 4:   Contemplating the Fifth 36
Chapter 5:   Contemplating the First 48
Chapter 6:   Contemplating the Second 67
Chapter 7:   Contemplating the Seventh 82
Chapter 8:   Contemplating the Eighth 109
Chapter 9:   Contemplating the Ninth 123
Chapter 10: The First Revelation of the
                Ninth Archetype of the Ninth Blessing –
                The Tenth Mountaintop Experience 129
Chapter 11: Contemplating a Vision of the Heavenly City
                Using the Rule of Sevens and Twelves 145
Chapter 12: Building My House Using the Rule of Nines 158
Epilogue: Contemplating the Nine Blessings 171
References 180

DEDICATION

To My Wife and Children
The Archetypes and Architects of My Blessings

PROLOGUE

COUNTING THE NINE BLESSINGS

1. *Blessed are the poor in spirit, for theirs is the kingdom of heaven.*
2. *Blessed are they who mourn, for they will be comforted.*
3. *Blessed are the meek, for they will inherit the land.*
4. *Blessed are they who hunger and thirst for righteousness, for they will be satisfied.*
5. *Blessed are the merciful, for they will be shown mercy.*
6. *Blessed are the clean of heart, for they will see God.*
7. *Blessed are the peacemakers, for they will be called children of God.*
8. *Blessed are they who are persecuted for the sake of righteousness, for theirs is the kingdom of heaven.*
9. *Blessed are you when they insult you and persecute you and utter every kind of evil against you [falsely] because of me. Rejoice and be glad, for your reward will be great in heaven.* [1]

---

[1] Mt 5:3-12

CHAPTER 1

CONTEMPLATING THE SIXTH

After six days Jesus took Peter, James, and John his brother, and led them up a high mountain by themselves. And he was transfigured before them; his face shone like the sun and his clothes became white as light. And behold, Moses and Elijah appeared to them, conversing with him. Then Peter said to Jesus in reply, "Lord, it is good that we are here. If you wish, I will make three tents here, one for you, one for Moses, and one for Elijah." While he was still speaking, behold, a bright cloud cast a shadow over them, then from the cloud came a voice that said, "This is my beloved Son, with whom I am well pleased; listen to him." When the disciples heard this, they fell prostrate and were very much afraid. But Jesus came and touched them, saying, "Rise, and do not be afraid." And when the disciples raised their eyes, they saw no one else but Jesus alone. As they were coming down from the mountain, Jesus charged them, "Do not tell the vision to anyone until the Son of Man has been raised from the dead." Then the disciples asked him, "Why do the scribes say that Elijah must come first?" He said in reply, "Elijah will indeed come and restore all things; but I tell you that Elijah has already come, and they did not recognize him but did to him whatever they pleased. So also will the Son of Man suffer at their hands." Then the disciples understood that he was speaking to them of John the Baptist. [2]

Autumn, circa AD 29: sunrise, either six days or eight days[3] after Peter confessed Jesus as the Messiah and Jesus first revealed His coming passion, at the southern base of Mount Herman of the Anti-Lebanon mountains, modern-day Israeli-occupied Golan Heights, formerly part of the Ottoman Empire, formerly of the Rashidun Caliphate, formerly Caesaria Phillipi of Herod Phillip II, formerly of Manasseh, the tribal patriarch, the first son of Joseph, grandson of Jacob, great-grandson of Isaac, and great, great-grandson of Abraham.

---

[2] Mt 17:1-13

[3] The Transfiguration follows several significant events in Matthew and Luke's Gospel. These include Peter's confession of Jesus as the Messiah and Jesus' first prediction of His passion. Mt 16:21-28 describes these events and then starts the description of the Transfiguration with the words, *"After six days."* Lk 9:18-27 describes these events and then starts its description of the Transfiguration with the words, "About eight days after he said this,"

The early morning light gently illuminates the base of Mount Hermon, casting long shadows and a soft glow over the rugged landscape. Jesus and his twelve disciples stir from their rest, the cool autumn air filled with the sounds of nature awakening. After a grueling six-day, one-hundred-kilometer trek from Caesarea Philippi, the group is weary but resolute. He had told them the night before,- "We have traveled here because we must ascend another very high mountain."

As they gather around a simple breakfast of fish and bread at the base of the imposing mountain, Jesus speaks with calm authority. He informs them that he, along with Peter, James, and John, will undertake the arduous eight-hour hike to the summit of Mount Hermon for an important meeting. The announcement is met with mixed reactions. Most of the nine remaining disciples feel a sense of relief, grateful to avoid the exhausting climb. They focus more on their meal than the implications of Jesus' words.

Matthew, however, is different. Over the past few years, he has meticulously chronicled Jesus' significant moments, especially those atop mountains. Most of the recordings take place in his keen mind, but he writes some of them down when circumstances allow. As he listens, he senses that something extraordinary is about to unfold. Catching Jesus' eye, he receives a subtle but unmistakable nod, a silent confirmation that his instincts are correct. This moment of understanding fills Matthew with a sense of anticipation. He sips the hot beverage, savoring its warmth, and recounts the previous five mountaintop experiences, mentally reviewing and quietly reflecting upon them. True, he and the other disciples only knew about some of the prior mountaintop experiences from Jesus' description. For instance, they had not been with him for the first, a notable exception in Matthew's opinion. Jesus' mother had described that one. Still, Matthew marvels at Jesus' exactitude, orderliness, and timing. Everything fits. He has followed him with the others. They had seen miraculous healings, the calming of the sea, the silencing of wind, and the demons. Indeed, they had heard that Sermon on the Mount, the third mountaintop experience, and discussed it. Talk about precision. Talk about the economy of words. Talk all you want, but all of yours and that talk of all the world could not produce the wisdom which flowed from his mouth on that day; yet, Matthew is certain he has barely started to recognize the full extent of that Sermon's wisdom.

Today, his mind races with curiosity and excitement. Just six days earlier, Jesus asked the disciples who people said he was, and Peter responded, *"You are the Messiah, the Son of the living God."*[4] Then Jesus explained how he must go to Jerusalem, suffer many things, be killed, and then be raised to life three days later. "Today, six days, three days? What," Matthew muses, "is the Master 'up to' today?" His head swirls as the unintended pun rushes into his thoughts, a testament to how naturally these thoughts now come to him. He doesn't ask for them. They just come. Slightly annoyed with himself for fussing over this inconsequential detail, he resolves to focus again on today, telling himself the scene is set for another profound chapter in their journey, and he must be ready to capture every detail when they return.

---

[4] Mt 16:16

Sunset, the same day

The evening air is crisp and cool as the disciples gather around a crackling campfire. The flames dance and flicker, casting a warm glow on their faces. James and John, the Brothers of Thunder, are animated, standing in front of the rest, as they recount the incredible event of the Transfiguration. The conversation is thoughtful but restrained; the three who were there, who saw and heard him, do not want to unintentionally misrepresent a single detail. James says slowly, "His face shone like the sun, and his clothes became white as light."

John picks up the description, "Fiery flame was emanating from Jesus' eyes, and the hair of His head was as white as wool."

Then, Peter speaks. "It wasn't until I asked about building tents that a bright cloud cast a shadow over us."

"A bright cloud?" asks Andrew. "Every cloud I've ever seen is dark."

"I know, brother," Peter replies, "This cloud was bright, I'm telling you, and filled with a divine presence."

"Is that why you wanted to build tents," asks Nathaniel.

"I don't know. I couldn't think of anything else to say, but then a voice from the cloud spoke. I never heard anything like it, I tell you."

After watching Peter struggle for a full minute to describe the voice, John breaks the silence and says, "The voice was like the sound of rushing water." As the description of the voice flows from John's mouth, Peter, James, and John stagger backward, struggling to remain standing, as the mere memory of hearing it smashes over them like a giant wave.

"What did it say," asks Thomas hesitantly. The three storytellers look at each other tentatively and silently agree that Peter should answer.

Peter steps forward, timidly in an uncharacteristic manner, and says, *"This is my beloved Son, with whom I am well pleased; listen to him,"* following which the three men fall to the ground, prostrate in front of Jesus.

No one speaks for another full minute until Jesus touches the three and says for the second time that day, *"Rise, and do not be afraid."*

Everyone stands. Matthew has said nothing the entire time. He has been listening intently, his mind racing as he processes the details. When he heard that Moses was present on the mountain, a shiver ran down his spine, quickly replaced by a surge of excitement. "I knew it," he thinks to himself. "I knew Moses would be up there." The sixth blessing echoes in his mind: *"Blessed are the clean of heart, for they shall **see** God."* [5] He emphasized and heard the word ***see,*** in his thoughts as if he needed to be reminded.

Matthew's thoughts turn to Moses, the great prophet who had seen God in so many ways. He recalls Moses' many encounters with the divine: the burning bush, his encounter with God on top of a burning and smoldering Mount Sinai, and the tent of meeting where God spoke to him face to face. When Moses left those tent meetings, his face shone so brightly that he had to cover it with a veil so the Israelites could look at him.

---

[5] Mt 5:8

"*Blessed are the clean of heart,*" Matthew repeats. "Moses, a man with the cleanest of hearts who had pleaded for Israel after the golden calf incident, had broken the tablets of the Ten Commandments and had fasted for forty days not once but twice. Moses, the man about whom scripture says, *Now the man Moses was very humble, more than anyone else on earth.* [6] Even more, Moses, about whom God reprimanded Aaron and Miriam, when he said, '*Now listen to my words: If there are prophets among you, in visions I reveal myself to them, in dreams I speak to them; Not so with my servant Moses! Throughout my house he is worthy of trust: face to face I speak to him, plainly and not in riddles. The likeness of the LORD he beholds.*'" [7]

"Indeed," Matthew marvels, "No one on earth had a heart as clean as Moses. Nor has anyone on earth seen God like Moses had. Yet Moses had not been content. '*Please let me see your glory,*' [8] he had asked."

Matthew continues, "But the Lord had responded, '*I will make all my goodness pass before you, and I will proclaim my name, 'LORD,' before you; I who show favor to whom I will, I who grant mercy to whom I will. But you cannot see my face, for no one can see me and live. Here is a place near me where you shall station yourself on the rock. When my glory passes, I will set you in the cleft of the rock and will cover you with my hand until I have passed by. Then I will*

---

[6] Nm 12:3
[7] Nm 12:6-8
[8] Ex 33:18

remove my hand, so that you may see my back; but my face may not be seen.'" [9]

Matthew thoughtfully reasoned, "This moment, even more than the one in which Moses learned he would not enter the Promised Land, must have been his saddest. He had longed to see the Lord's face, his glory."

As this idea settles on Matthew, he looks up and sees Jesus on the other side of the campfire, his face shining as the flames dance in his eyes. The others are filtering out to find a place to sleep. Jesus looks back at Matthew and catches Matthew looking at Him; His eyes look right through Matthew, piercing his heart and causing him to melt inside. Awe-stricken, Matthew wonders, "Have I seen God's glory?"

Another shudder, a thrill, rocks Matthew to his core. He murmurs to himself, "Moses, dear Moses. You saw God today. You saw his face today. Your request to see God's glory was fulfilled today. Yes, dear Moses, today, at last, you saw God. You saw all of God today on that mountain. You saw his glory today, fifteen hundred years after asking." Matthew looked up to see that face again, but Jesus had turned to join the others to find a place to sleep. Sleep comes quickly upon the cozy group. Matthew lies on his back, eyes wide, staring at the stars, wondering, marveling, praying. "Lord, I pray, show me your glory."

---

[9] Ex 33:19-23

CHAPTER 2

CONTEMPLATING THE THIRD

When he saw the crowds, he went up the mountain, and after he had sat down, his disciples came to him. He began to teach them, saying: [10]

Late afternoon circa AD 27: the Mount of the Beatitudes a short walk from a small hill 24 meters above sea level, nearly 215 meters above the Sea of Galilee on its northwestern shore, near Capernaum and the southern slopes of the Korazim Plateau, modern-day Franciscan Chapel where Pope John Paul II celebrated Mass on March 24, 2000, formerly the site of a 4th-century Byzantine church.

---

[10] Mt 5:1-2

Matthew is sitting on a rock in the late afternoon, listening to the breeze gently rustling the leaves on the olive trees around him and reflecting on the day's profound teachings. He hears a deep rumble and feels a soft droplet of rain on his forehead. The splash is tender, almost like a whisper from the heavens. He looks up to see the sky, now overcast, releasing a delicate shower. The cool water begins to run over his head, trickling through his hair and down his face, mingling with the sweat and dust of the day's journey. It is refreshing, a soothing balm after the intense afternoon heat. The rain grows steadier, and Matthew sees a visible stream forming, a thin, shimmering sheet of water cascading down from the sky. He closes his eyes, letting the rain wash over him, feeling a sense of calm and renewal. It is as if the rain is a physical manifestation of the spiritual cleansing and new beginning that Jesus had spoken of.

As he replays the scene in his mind, he listens again to the echoes of Jesus' voice, resonating with authority and compassion. Many of the Sermon's words filtered past. However, the words *Blessed are the meek, for they shall inherit the earth,* [11] linger. He senses that he is missing something, some other vital meaning, plainly stated but hidden, tucked away, in plain sight, manifest conspicuously but not appreciated, not by himself, and not by the others. He recalls Jesus saying he would start something new today shortly before starting the Sermon. No, the word he used was "recreate." Matthew ponders this. "Recreate what: everything or everyone? Recreate when: today, tomorrow, or next week? As far

---

[11] Mt 5:5

as he could tell, nothing had changed, at least not visibly, not in any way plainly manifest to his senses."

He had asked Jesus in private, "Lord, what did you do on that little hill today?"

Jesus had responded with a look that seemed to say, "Surely you know what I'm talking about." Matthew had felt a mix of confusion and curiosity.

Not long after this, he began taking notes whenever he could, making a journal to capture the essence of his travels with Jesus and the growing band of followers.

Jesus had teased him, "You are behind already, my carefully counting ex-tax collector- this is my third mountaintop experience."

"Well, it's my first with you, Jesus," Matthew had replied. "Please tell me about the first two."

"I will," said Jesus, "but let me explain more about this third one. I can see the confusion on your face." Then Jesus repeated, *"Blessed are the meek, for they shall inherit the earth."* He had looked at Matthew with a knowing smile again. He asked, "Tell me, Matthew, who among every person who ever walked the earth, except for the couple that God used to start humanity, who with their progeny would inherit a newly created earth?" Matthew had no answer. He realized that Jesus was speaking of a deeper, spiritual recreation, a regeneration that wasn't immediately visible to the eye but was transformative, nonetheless.

Matthew looks up again and sees the rain droplets merging into sheets, creating a continuous flow that dances in the air before meeting the Earth. The sound of the rain is a gentle symphony, each drop adding to the melody of nature. The world around him seems to come alive, the colors of the grass and trees more vibrant, the air filling with the fresh, earthy scent of rain. At that moment, he feels a deep connection to the teachings of the day, and a profound sense of peace settles over him. Matthew is thrilled, thinking he has completely cracked the code and understood the meaning of Jesus' Sermon on the Mount. He makes a mental note to jot down the words he will write someday in a lengthy account of these days with Jesus.

"I've got it, Jesus," he nearly shouts, startling the rest of the group. "I understand this new creation of which you speak." These words caught the attention of John, the young one who, despite his youth, shared a wonderful propensity for spiritual insights, for seeing the divine purpose in the everyday events of life.

"Yes, Jesus, a realization has dawned on me, excuse the pun, that the new creation of which you spoke has already begun in the hearts of those who listen to and believe you."

A hushed silence follows. Every pair of eyes shifts from Matthew to Jesus. What would the master say? Jesus smiles and opens his mouth to speak, but after a moment, he closes his mouth, opens his eyes wide, and shifts his gaze upwards, heavenwards.

At that very moment, the sun breaks through the clouds, through the gentle rain. Then, Jesus redirects his gaze from the sunny opening through the clouds to the horizon opposite it; all eyes follow his eyes until all see it: a magnificent rainbow, gloriously stretched across the horizon, its colors merging. A full minute passes without a word, profound silence, save for a distant rumble, a gentle breeze, a steady flow of rain so monotonous it fades out of hearing.

Then, Jesus speaks. "Yes, Matthew, you have understood part of the third blessing I spoke about today. But not all of it. Think with me, my dear disciples. Ask the question again. Who, among all your descendants, literally, not only spiritually, but literally and actually inherited a new earth?" Another full minute of silence follows.

Then the young disciple, with his gaze still fixed on the rainbow, speaks; his voice is awe-filled and earnest, far too weighty for a man his age. Filled with supernatural conviction, he proclaims, "That man is Noah."

Immediately, the once quiet dozen erupts into a symphony of their own, their voices creating a melody of truth, leaving them both awestruck and contemplative. Peter stands and speaks.

"Brothers, Noah and his family opened the hatch of the ark, sitting atop Mount Ararat, after living in it for a year, and beheld the entire earth they had just inherited."

"And God confirmed it with the sign of the rainbow," adds John. "Recall," he continues, "how Noah built an altar to the LORD on which he offered burnt offerings of every clean animal and every clean bird. The crucial word here is 'clean.' Like Abel, who brought the fatty portion of the firstlings of his flock, Noah sacrificed the best for the Lord. And, like Adam, who was called to learn humility by laboring over the soil, Noah was called to learn humility through the work God assigned to him."

Jesus was thrilled to see and hear such things from his new disciples, especially the youngest, who was already advancing to the front in terms of understanding earthly truths spiritually. Jesus knew it would not always be like this, that they would be slow to understand more difficult things. Still wanting to nurture the truths growing within them, he quotes a section from Genesis. *"When the LORD smelled the sweet odor, the LORD said to himself:*

Never again will I curse the ground because of human beings, since the desires of the human heart are evil from youth; nor will I ever again strike down every living being, as I have done. All the days of the earth, seedtime and harvest, cold and heat, Summer and winter, and day and night shall not cease." [12]

Silence follows until Matthew speaks. "Lord, Noah inherited the earth; better still, an earth that now existed with a promise from God to sustain forever. That's the second part of the Beatitude. Please explain to us his meekness. What did Noah have or do that qualified him to inherit it?"

Jesus answers. "To understand Noah's meekness, we must consider him before this post-flood incident. Genesis describes him, *But Noah found favor with the LORD. These are the descendants of Noah. Noah was a righteous man and blameless in his generation; Noah walked with God.* [13] In these verses, Genesis describes Noah favorably four times. Noah found favor with God, one; was righteous and blameless, two and three; and walked with God, four."

"Ok," Peter muses, "but Genesis tells us that Enoch also walked with God and repeated it a second time. Therefore, can we assume that, like Noah, Enoch was a righteous and blameless man who found favor with God?"

James speaks. "Yes, God's taking Enoch seems to reflect the desires of God's heart for all children who walk with him in a sin-filled world."

"He wants to take them home to heaven to be with Him forever," John concludes.

---

[12] Gn 8:21-22
[13] Gn 6:8-9

Jesus answers. "Very good observations, Peter, James, and John. Still, we are left with Matthew's question. It is clear from the story that God had different plans for Noah. He had work for Noah to do. Through Noah's response to God's commands, we learn the kind of man he was and why God considered him righteous. First, consider the incredible things God asked of Noah, which we can read about in Genesis. We learn the details of the rather large task God placed before him. To summarize the task, God told him to build a huge ark and gather two of every kind of animal that crawls on the ground and birds of the air so that Noah can keep them alive- not a small or easy task. He also told Noah to gather enough food to feed them and his family for a long time. Please note Noah's response. *Noah complied; he did just as God had commanded him.* [14] After this, Noah received another command from God: *Of every clean animal, take with you seven pairs, a male and its mate; and of the unclean animals, one pair, a male and its mate; likewise, of every bird of the air, seven pairs, a male and a female, to keep their progeny alive over all the earth."* [15]

Jesus pauses, waits for their looks of understanding, and continues. "After receiving this not-so-small commandment, Noah received some not-too-good news when God said: *For seven days from now I will bring rain down on the earth for forty days and forty nights, and so I will wipe out from the face of the earth every being that I have made.* [16] It is easy to miss the enormity of the situation God placed before Noah. Still, Noah's response,

---

[14] Gn 6:22
[15] Gn 7:2-3
[16] Gn 7:4

meaning his actions, tells the story. We can't help seeing the word repeated. *Noah complied, just as the LORD had commanded.* [17] It is in the word comply that we find the meaning of meekness."

Again, Jesus pauses. He wants to make sure they don't miss this point. "Friends, people often mistakenly think meekness conveys the idea of weakness, but it misses the word's true meaning. Meekness means just the opposite of weakness. It means strength and confidence, but here is the key. It means strength and confidence through reliance on God. Further, we are talking about a very active reliance on God, far from a passive verbal ascent. We see this in the word complied, a conjunction of two words, ' com,' meaning with, and 'ply,' meaning to work vigorously. Noah's compliance with God portrays a man who worked hard with God. He worked as a man with a mission. The half-hearted or weak-willed man could not have complied with God like Noah or completed the humanly impossible task God gave him. He worked feverishly, no doubt, but he could not have complied in this manner unless he was a supremely meek man who knew complete dependence on God. By his meekness, Noah found the strength and no doubt the grace of God to complete a humanly impossible task, and for his meekness, Noah found favor with God, and for that, God gave him the entire earth. Not bad for a year's work."

As Jesus finished his explanation, the clouds covered the sun for the last time that day. The rainbow disappeared, promising to return another day, and Matthew writes in his journal. "The third one explained, eight more to go."

---

[17] Gn 7:5

CHAPTER 3

CONTEMPLATING THE FOURTH

Then he made the disciples get into the boat and precede him to the other side, while he dismissed the crowds. After doing so, he went up on the mountain by himself to pray. When it was evening he was there alone. [18]

Early dawn, circa AD 28: on a boat in the Sea of Galilee heading towards the town of Gennesaret

In the dim light of early dawn, the boat rocks gently on the calm waters of the Sea of Galilee. The disciples, still catching their breath, sit in stunned silence. Moments ago, they had witnessed something beyond their comprehension: Jesus walking on water,

---

[18] Mt 14:22-23

and then Peter, too, stepping out in faith only to be saved by Jesus' steady hand when he faltered. The air is thick with awe and reverence, each disciple's mind racing with questions and wonder. Who is this man who walks on water, feeds five thousand men and their families with a few loaves and fish, and then gathers twelve baskets of leftovers, one basket for each of the twelve disciples? Matthew noted that detail, not only because Jesus handed him his basket last but because he counts things like that routinely. He had also counted the loaves and fish given to Jesus to bless before feeding the multitude. There were five loaves and two fish. He had done the math, recalled Jesus' instructions to have the crowd sit in groups of fifty, and multiplied that by 100 to calculate 5000. A young boy and a few others were all too happy to run around counting the groups. "I counted one hundred groups," the lad had said. "You are a good lad; Matthew had commended him. I hope you will continue to use your counting skills for good."

The mood had lightened significantly as this miracle unfolded, but alone in the boat after witnessing the water walking, their hearts were heavy again with the news of John the Baptist's brutal death, a sorrow that had yet to be voiced. Matthew, in particular, had seen the deep sadness in Jesus' eyes earlier that day. He had wanted to offer comfort, but Jesus had gone up the mountain by himself, and the rapid succession of miraculous events had left no room for words. Now, in the quiet of the boat, the disciples marvel at the compassion and power of their teacher. Jesus had shown them, through his actions, a love that transcends grief and a power that defies nature. The miraculous feeding, the walking on water, and the saving of Peter were all profound demonstrations of His divine authority and boundless compassion. The disciples sit in silent reflection, their hearts filling with awe, reverence, and a deepening understanding of the one they follow.

Matthew's presence could have been easily missed even in that small, crowded boat. He was so focused on the significance of that fourth mountaintop experience. He said nothing, but he had done some pondering after the Sermon on the Mount. Jesus said that was the third mountain of significance and had brought to light how that Sermon, the third of nine to come, should be associated with Noah. Matthew had asked why not Moses. Had Jesus not come as another Moses, giving a new law. Was he not fulfilling what Moses started when he gave the first law in the tablets? Jesus assured him that Moses could and should be associated with the Sermon on the Mount and many other parts of his mission in the future. However, Moses's special mountaintop experience was still to come.

So then, Matthew ponders, if Moses is yet to come and someone is to follow Noah, who does that leave? What man should we associate with His fourth mountaintop experience? He looks towards the approaching shoreline, surrounded by hills and lush vegetation, and spots a few herons gliding effortlessly over the water. He sees an apple orchard and feels his stomach churn. As he quietly asks himself the question, he absentmindedly pulls the last small fragment of bread from his basket and chews. As he chews, Father Abraham suddenly comes to mind, and an idea flashes before him. He gasps out loud, startling the others. As the idea takes hold in his mind, his mouth dries up.

The bread he had just tried to swallow remains stuck in his mouth, hanging over two internal orifices, one that leads to his stomach and another to his lungs, and then it moves just under his epiglottis into the wrong orifice. His face turns red as his supply of air is cut off. He starts to panic. He wants to cough but can't. He needs air to do that. He suddenly stands up, rocking the boat, catching everyone's attention. A few shout, "Be careful! Are you trying to tip us?"

Simon, known as the Zealot, is next to him. He sees and understands that Matthew is choking. He stands up, causing the boat to lurch still further, and more dismayed voices are heard. Simon bends Matthew forward and slaps his back vigorously. A few moments later, Matthew starts coughing. After a series of increasingly forceful coughs, the bread is propelled back into his mouth. As he inhales deeply, everyone breathes a sigh of relief, and the two sit back down.

Matthew looks at Jesus, who has just opened his eyes, and yawns. He slept through the entire incident. Now, he smiles at Matthew. He doesn't say a word, but Matthew knows what to do next. He would have done the same thing anyway, given his propensity not to waste anything, especially the last morsel from the miraculous feeding. Matthew chews again. He chews some more and swallows hard but can't swallow the bread. His mouth is completely dry and devoid of any saliva. He hasn't drunk water for several hours at sea under a hot sun. And, his mouth is dry for another reason. A dry mouth can follow a shocking thought as it did in this case when he made the association of Father Abraham with the fourth Beatitude.

Silently, Jesus hands Matthew his leather pouch. Matthew takes a sip, his eyes fixed on Jesus, drinking thankfully. As the last of the cool water carries the bread into his stomach, he notes a subtle but definite change in the water's taste. Is that wine

Jesus has just given him, but how? They had filled their pouches with water right before taking their seats in the boat. Has he just repeated the miracle he had performed at the wedding? Matthew was about to say something, about to ask Jesus a question, but the Master spoke first.

"What do you think, Matthew? Does not Abraham fit the bill? Can you think of anyone else so qualified to be called the Archetype of the Fourth Blessing?"

Flushed with the excitement of sharing his thoughts and flushed from the effects of the fluid entering his bloodstream, he opens his mouth to speak.

However, before Matthew can speak, Nathanael speaks. "Remind us, Lord, what was the fourth blessing."

Matthew was preparing to quote it, but before he could say a word, Andrew, Peter's brother, says, *"Blessed are they who hunger and thirst for righteousness, for they will be satisfied."* [19]

"Well said, Andrew," says Jesus, "and do you see why it fits with Abraham?"

Matthew jumps to his feet, prepared to answer, causing the boat to list his way.

"Don't jump up like that," several shout. He sits down abruptly. In the meantime, James, the son of Alphaeus, raises his hand to speak. Exacerbated, Matthew keeps his mouth shut and listens with the rest.

"Lord," begins the one also known as James the Lesser, "Genesis tells the story of Abraham's test, how, after years of struggle, God

---

[19] Mt 5:6

provided Isaac, provided the son through whom God would fulfill the promise he made to Abraham to make him a father of many nations."

He pauses. Matthew jumps at the chance to speak, figuratively and literally. Another chorus of "Sit down" follows. "Ok," says Matthew, "but I must say something."

"You will get your chance. Please don't jump up again," says Judas Iscariot.

James, the son of Zebedee, then speaks. "I like where this is going. Abraham loved nothing and no one more than Isaac, yet when God told him to sacrifice him, Abraham obeyed."

"Yes, but,…" Matthew interjected.

"Yes, but he obeyed because he believed God would provide the lamb for the sacrifice," adds Philip before Matthew can finish his sentence.

"Yes, and in case anyone doubts his intention to carry on with the sacrifice of his beloved son, he even raised his hand, dagger in hand, to kill the son, bound up and laying on the wood pile to be consumed by the living God," says Thomas without a moment's hesitation.

"Yes, yes, I know," says Matthew, but there is more."

"Oh, yes, there is more," says Thaddeus.

"He had obeyed God for many years," chimes in Peter.

"Indeed, Abraham trusted God, hungered and thirsted for God's righteousness that strongly, beyond what any of us would dare to conceive," concludes Simon the Zealot.

"Correct, all of you," Jesus says, "And God satisfied Abraham's hunger and thirst by providing the Lamb. Recall the words from Genesis, 'Do not lay your hand on the boy,' said the angel. 'Do not *do the least thing to him. For now I know that you fear God, since you did not withhold from me your son, your only one.' Abraham looked up and saw a single ram caught by its horns in the thicket. So Abraham went and took the ram and offered it up as a burnt offering in place of his son. Abraham named that place Yahweh-yireh; hence people today say, 'On the mountain the LORD will provide.'* [20]

In fact, at that moment, God elevated the promise he had made to Abraham to an oath. Hear the words that follow from Genesis. *A second time the angel of the LORD called to Abraham from heaven and said: 'I swear by my very self—oracle of the LORD—that because you acted as you did in not withholding from me your son, your only one, I will bless you and make your descendants as countless as the stars of the sky and the sands of the seashore; your descendants will take possession of the gates of their enemies, and in your descendants all the nations of the earth will find blessing, because you obeyed my command.'"* [21]

A long, stunned silence follows, every disciple processing Jesus' words. Matthew is so stunned by what he has just heard that he forgets what he wants to say. That bothers him. It bothers him a lot because he knows what he wants to say is important for the discussion. Still, for whatever reason, the thoughts escape him. He looks at Jesus, who doesn't say anything. However, he hands Matthew his leather bag again.

Matthew takes another drink, and then his eyes light up. "Can I speak now, Lord?" "Please do," says Jesus with a smile; "only stay seated."

---

[20] Gn 22:12-14
[21] Gn 22:15-18

Matthew suppresses the urge to stand and begins to share his thoughts. "Lord, I think there was another incident in Abraham's life that can be understood as qualifying him to be the Archetype of the Fourth Blessing."

"Go on, please tell us, oh thoughtful one," says Jesus.

"I was thinking, Lord of Abraham's, well actually, Abram's interactions with Melchizedek about twenty-five years before this incident with Isaac, soon after God first singled him out and commanded him to leave the land of his family and to go to Egypt. Abram's nephew Lot had set up his family near Sodom and had been taken captive by the four kings who had been victorious over five other kings. When Abram heard of Lot's capture, he mustered three hundred men and retrieved Lot and all his possessions. In this way, he hungered mightily for righteousness. He would not leave his nephew and his family to be used and violated by their captors. Instead, he risked his life, trusting God to help him fight the battle."

Matthew pauses momentarily to take a breath after the continuous pouring forth of words. "Beautiful, Matthew," says Jesus. "Tell us how God satisfied his hunger and thirst for righteousness."

Matthew takes a deep breath and says, "Well, Lord, in this case, God worked through another man; at least, I think he was a man. His name was Melchizedek. Recall what he said and did. Let me quote the words from the scroll for all of you." And then, before anyone could interrupt, he said, *"Melchizedek, king of Salem, brought out bread and wine. He was a priest of God Most High. He blessed Abram with these words: 'Blessed be Abram by God Most High, the creator of heaven and earth; And blessed be God Most High, who delivered your foes into your hand.' Then Abram gave him a tenth of everything.'"* [22] Matthew stops speaking just as suddenly as he had started, looking around at the others with a smile, waiting for his words to have their effect.

A second, long, stunned silence follows. No one speaks; each lost, as it were, or we can say, 'found' in thought by a wonderful, miraculous, crazy, and unexpected truth, thinking and counting the blessings. They had arrived at the Fourth Blessing and found its Archetype. John, the only one who had not spoken, ponders deeply the meaning of Melchizedek's bread and wine. He doesn't say anything, allowing the words and the day's events to rest quietly within a growing mystical catalog of thoughts he would share later when he writes about his time with Jesus. For the remainder of the trip across the sea, no one speaks. No one says a thing. No one moves, not even Matthew, who has no reason to jump up. No one notices until it is time to disembark that they have arrived on the shores of Gennesaret. Jesus gets out and walks ahead of the group. Matthew watches and says to himself, "Someday, I will write it like this; *when the men of that place recognized him, they sent word to all the surrounding country. People brought to him all those who were sick and begged him that they might touch only the tassel on his cloak, and as many as touched it were healed.*" [23]

The disciples get out of the boat and watch as Jesus allows himself to be caught up in the crowd, to be within a suffering mass of humanity. What should they say? What could they have said? What should they do? What can they do? What would they do? A new day is upon them. They get out of the boat. There is work to be done.

---

[22] Gn 14:18-20
[23] Mt 14:35-36

CHAPTER 4

CONTEMPLATING THE FIFTH

Moving on from there Jesus walked by the Sea of Galilee, went up on the mountain, and sat down there. [24]

Part One

Mid-afternoon, circa AD 28: about one or two days after the fourth mountaintop experience, rehashing food-related experiences on a mountain on the northwest shore of the Sea of Galilee

They are on the trail, having just filled their water pouches; they start the hot trek down the other side of the mountain. Jesus is

---

[24] Mt 15:29

far ahead of the group, followed by Andrew and Nathaniel, and the other nine follow. Matthew lags behind, the last, as usual. He watches a small gecko scutter under a rock as a black raven flies overhead. The rhythm of wildlife fascinates him more each day spent with these simple, salt-of-the-earth men, a stark contrast with his days as a city-dweller. He has some self-awareness of his idiosyncrasies, that he tends to be compulsive about details most find unnecessary at best and frankly boring at worst. He is aware that he will often hyperfocus on a topic, looking at it from every angle, analyzing it over and over, double, no triple, no quadruple, checking his train of thoughts from the start to their conclusion. So what? These qualities served him well in his days as a tax collector. Jesus didn't ask him to shutter up his talents; He did the opposite. The only change Jesus asked concerned his attitude and his end purpose. Give to people instead of taking. Love people instead of remaining aloof and indifferent. He candidly admits he has a long way to go on that front. Besides, given his choking experience just a few days ago as Jesus facilitated a group discussion that led to some astounding ideas about Abraham as the Archetype of that Sermon's Fourth Blessing; yes, given all of this, one could hardly blame him for lagging behind the rest of the group for some quiet, for yet another opportunity to catalog the events surrounding that fourth mountaintop experience, and yes to observe the wildlife.

Truthfully, some of the parables Jesus had told as they made their way to Nazareth seem to serve as preliminary lessons. "Why," he imagines himself explaining to the others, "because they are concerned with food. There are three parables about sowing seed: one that focuses on the need for it to be planted in rich soil to reap much fruit, another that focuses on how weeds would grow up with the wheat, and a third about the mustard seed, a small seed producing an abundant harvest. And don't forget the woman who mixed yeast with three measures of wheat flour until the whole batch was leavened." He wasn't sure how to interpret that one. He wonders about the significance of it being 'three measures.' He continues the catalog, the silent monologue. "After the disappointment of being rejected in his native place, Jesus had moved on and, before long, received the news of John the Baptist's beheading. Had Herodias really asked for it to be brought into the banquet hall on a platter? Talk about a bad food image. It wasn't long after this news that Jesus fed the five thousand. Bad images, good images juxtaposed, wheat and weeds, and other food-related images; this Jesus said is the kingdom of heaven. Obviously, I am missing something."

Matthew pauses his cataloging to inspect a patch of yellow flowers and the bees darting in and out of them. "Amazing creatures," he thinks. "Do they really help flowers spread from one place to the next?" Returning to the matter on his mind, he says to himself, "The fourth mountaintop experience followed the beheading. Jesus climbed that mountain alone. Now, here on the fifth, everyone is making the trek. Yes, and today started like so many others. The early risers rose first. The heavy sleepers slumbered until they smelled breakfast cooking. An interesting and, again, food-related conversation ensued. Some Pharisees from Jerusalem had joined them. It seemed innocent enough until they started asking pointed questions. Matthew remembered leading the conversation with the disciples after breakfast and asking, "Has anyone considered our Lord's interactions with the elders? Let me remind you. They started things by asking, *Why do your disciples break the tradition of the elders? They do not wash [their] hands when they eat a meal.* Remember how Jesus responded, *And why do you break the commandment of God for the sake of your tradition?* Remember, things went from bad to worse when Jesus summoned the crowd to explain, *It is not what enters one's mouth that defiles that person; but what comes out of the mouth is what defiles one."* [25]

Matthew interrupts his own mental catalog to ask himself a question. "Why does it always return to food, eating, and the like?" He recalls Peter demonstrating again his challenge with understanding the spiritual messages behind some of Jesus' teachings. He recalls Peter asking Jesus to explain the parable about what does and what does not defile a person. And he recalls Jesus' response. *"Are even you still without understanding? Do you not realize that everything that enters the mouth passes into the stomach and is expelled into the latrine? But the things that come out of the mouth come from the heart, and they defile. For from the heart come evil thoughts, murder, adultery, unchastity, theft, false witness, blasphemy. These are what defile a person, but to eat with unwashed hands does not defile."* [26]

Matthew continues his silent trek down the mountain. He walks carefully around a narrow rocky bend in the path. As the path widens, Matthew trots ahead to catch the rest of the group but slows down again to pass through a steep, narrow, curvy hatchback trail. Focusing carefully on the path directly ahead, meaning where his feet will fall, he navigates past a few steep

---

[25] Mt 15:2, 3, and 11
[26] Mt 15:16-20

ledges and then reaches a wider section leading to the mountain's base. He catches up with the others who are sitting.

"Oh, Peter," Matthew says quietly, "why does Jesus look at you as if He has a special leadership role in mind for you? Have you yet realized He has called us to fish for men?"

Peter chuckles but doesn't answer. Save for a few small laughs, the others remain quiet. John smiles and remains silent. Matthew lets that line of thinking go to resume his musings, bringing everyone into the conversation as if they had all heard the monologue he has been having alone since the trek began hours before. In truth, they had heard it before, not on this day, but on many others.

"You see, brothers, it always comes down to food," while placing a bit of bread he had saved from breakfast in his mouth. Someone clears their throat loudly and mimics forceful coughing.

Nathaniel nods toward Matthew's water pouch and says, "Take a drink, brother. We don't want to see you passing out here, though I suspect those vultures circling overhead would have their own food-related conversation while feasting on you."

Drinking water and laughing, Matthew says, "I thought I had come to the end of the catalog of food-related events and teachings, but then I recalled the interaction with the Canaanite women. Brothers, can I ask a question? Did Jesus really say to her, *It is not right to take the food of the children and throw it to the dogs,* and did that Canaanite woman really say to Jesus, *Please, Lord, for even the dogs eat the scraps that fall from the table of their masters?* And did Jesus really say and do what I heard? *O woman, great is your faith!* [27] *Let it be done for you as you wish.' And her daughter was healed from that hour."*

They look up and watch a vulture part from the other three and circle towards a carcass two hundred or so yards from the group. The other vultures soon follow. Interrupting the silence, Peter asks, "As she wished? Are you sure you heard that right? Do you want her to eat scraps like these vultures?"

"No, Peter," Simon the Zealot answers, "He wants her to eat the scraps like those jackals." He points to five of them running hither and thro, alternating from a brave advance and a fearful retreat from the imposing birds of prey.

Matthew watches in fascination another new encounter away from civilization and cities, another encounter with the barren boondocks, the remote hinterland, the uncivilized wilderness. Breaking free from his thoughts, he says, "Peter, her daughter was healed. That is what she came to Jesus for."

"Here they come again," Thomas says. They all look up and then stand up.

They see Jesus one-hundred-fifty meters ahead. They watch Him move forward as *"great crowds came to him, having with them the lame, the blind, the deformed, the mute, and many others. They placed them at his feet, and he cured them."* [28]

"Here we go again," says Philip, who never tires of seeing the crowds and the miracles. They all enjoy seeing this and are all re-amazed. It just seems that Philip is often the first to get excited

---

[27] Mt 15:22-28
[28] Mt 15:30

about it. "Wait, what is Jesus doing now," says Philip, moving forward as:

"Jesus summoned his disciples and said, 'My heart is moved with pity for the crowd, for they have been with me now for three days and have nothing to eat. I do not want to send them away hungry, for fear they may collapse on the way.' The disciples said to him, 'Where could we ever get enough bread in this deserted place to satisfy such a crowd?' Jesus said to them, 'How many loaves do you have?' 'Seven,' they replied, 'and a few fish.' He ordered the crowd to sit down on the ground. Then he took the seven loaves and the fish, gave thanks, broke the loaves, and gave them to the disciples, who in turn gave them to the crowds. They all ate and were satisfied. They picked up the fragments left over—seven baskets full. Those who ate were four thousand men, not counting women and children." [29]

Matthew thinks, "Food, food, food- it always comes down to food and eating."

Part Two

The evening after feeding four thousand in the district of Magadan

Jesus and His disciples recline under a clear star-filled sky, finishing their meals, enjoying fellowship, and discussing the food-related catalog of events Matthew has shared with them. "Matthew," Jesus says, "It was good of you to think through all of that. You might

---

[29] Mt 15:32-38

want to do the same for the other and future intra-mountaintop experiences. Please take note. The Nine Blessings from the Sermon on the Mount should not be considered isolated truths. Rather, one truth leads into the next and vice versa. I am building human character, and those truths should move seamlessly from one to the other and back again. You cannot be a man who hungers and thirsts for righteousness unless you have first become a humble man who mourns his sin and meekly depends on God for everything in life."

Matthew doesn't say a word but remembers what John had said about Noah imitating Able and Adam. John is always ahead of the curve when it comes to seeing the spiritual side. He wishes he had that gift. Now, his mind is reeling at the thought of organizing and chronically the events of those other intra-mountaintop experiences. It is dark. Still, he wonders if he should try to write some notes by the firelight. No, that won't work. It feels overwhelming, and to make matters worse, he can do nothing about it right now. Then, he recalls a question he has chewed over for some time.

"Lord," he begins, "none of us was there for the first and second mountaintop experiences. How can I catalog those events?"

Jesus responds, "I will tell you about the first, and my mother will tell you about the second when the time is right. However, before getting into the first or second, we must look at what you have missed today concerning the fifth because you focused your thoughts on the fourth instead of living in the moment as we climbed up and down the fifth mountain."

It was a gentle rebuke, but it was one Matthew would try to remember. Jesus had assured him and the others that they would recall whatever they needed to recall when the time to recall it arrived. The Holy Spirit would help with that. Still, it is hard for Matthew to do this, with his obsessive-compulsive tendencies. He did not find it easy to 'let go and let live,' as they say.

"Anyone here," Jesus begins, "please repeat the first sentence of the Canaanite women." "Of course, Lord," says Peter. *"Have pity on me, Lord, Son of David!"* [30]

"Correct, Peter," says Jesus. "All of you should pay attention to the Son of David part as we continue our journey towards his city. However, right now, I want to focus on *Have pity on me.* Pitying someone should and usually does motivate us to show mercy to that person. Peter, quote the Fifth Blessing."

"Blessed are the merciful, for they shall be shown mercy," [31] Peter says, as he winks at Matthew, "Not bad for a simple fisherman, eh?" He continues, "Still, Lord, to be perfectly candid, none of us responded very well. Her persistence bothered us until you, Lord, corrected our attitude by showing compassion towards her."

"Yes, brother," adds Andrew, "the Lord spelled it out for us a bit later after healing many of the lame and sick. He said, *My heart is moved with pity for the crowd, for they have been with me now for three days and have nothing to eat. I do not want to send them away hungry, for fear they may collapse on the way."* [32]

"Which brings us to a question, Lord," says Matthew. "Who is the Archetype of the Fifth Blessing?" As he asks the question, he looks around at the others only to see blank stares. He is tempted

---

[30] Mt 15:22
[31] Mt 5:7
[32] Mt 15:32

to remind them that his musings have not been for naught entirely. However, there was one big problem. He doesn't know the answer, but he does share his thoughts.

"Logically, one could deduce that this Archetype of the Fifth Blessing has to be a man who lived after Abraham. Could it be Isaac? Isaac had received mercy at the last minute? Could it be Jacob? Perhaps because he, after all, had some unique and remarkable God experiences. What about that dream where he saw a stairway resting on the ground, its top reaching the heavens, and God's angels were going up and down on it? Might that dream hold some interpretive key to understanding the Nine Blessings?"

"I agree, Matthew," says Nathaniel, "but something about Jacob doesn't feel right. Yes, Jacob ended up receiving the name Israel, and it was from him that the twelve tribes of Israel descended. But, still, Jacob, the deceiver, lined up next to Noah and Abraham. It just doesn't feel right?"

Jesus claps and says, "And all this insight comes from the man who knows no guile."

"Well, Lord," Matthew says, "that leads us to Jacob's twelve sons."

"Correct, Matthew. Let me get right to the point. Have you considered Joseph?" Questioning murmurs, short, hushed conversations, and a single 'a ha' follow.

The 'a ha' came from John, the youngest among them and perhaps the most qualified to comment on this second to the youngest son of Jacob. "I've got it. Do you remember Joseph's story? The older brothers, jealous of his favored status with their father, threw him into a well. He is fished out and taken captive to Egypt, where because of his remarkable dream interpreting skills and wisdom, he eventually earns the most trusted role in Pharaoh's kingdom. Fast forward to a severe famine, Joseph's wise management of grain, and the subsequent journey of those same evil brothers to Egypt to find critical provisions. At that point, Joseph, whom they did not recognize, had every reason and motivation to ignore their request. Who would blame him for giving them an eye for an eye type of treatment, but he didn't. The story of how he led them from fearing for their lives to receiving mercy from him is one of the most touching stories in the Torah. Joseph loved his brothers despite the evil way they treated him. He showed mercy where most would have exacted revenge. Listen carefully as I recite words that so poignantly reveal his feelings.

Joseph could no longer restrain himself in the presence of all his attendants, so he cried out, 'Have everyone withdraw from me!' So no one attended him when he made himself known to his brothers. But his sobs were so loud that the Egyptians heard him, and so the news reached Pharaoh's house. 'I am Joseph,' he said to his brothers. 'Is my father still alive?' But his brothers could give him no answer, so dumbfounded were they at him. 'Come closer to me,' Joseph told his brothers. When they had done so, he said: 'I am your brother Joseph, whom you sold into Egypt. But now do not be distressed, and do not be angry with yourselves for having sold me here. It was really for the sake of saving lives that God sent me here ahead of you. The famine has been in the land for two years now, and for five more years cultivation will yield no harvest. God, therefore, sent me on ahead of you to ensure for you a remnant on earth and to save your lives in an extraordinary deliverance. So it was not really you but God who had me come here; and he has made me a father to Pharaoh, Lord of all his household, and ruler over the whole land of Egypt. Hurry back, then, to my father and tell him: 'Thus says your son Joseph: God has made me Lord of all Egypt; come down to me without delay. You can settle in the region of Goshen, where you will be near me—you and your children and children's children, your flocks and herds, and everything that you own. I will provide for you there in the five years of famine that lie ahead, so that you and your household and all that are yours will not suffer want.' Surely, you can see for yourselves, and Benjamin can see for himself, that it is I who am speaking to you. Tell my father all about my high position in Egypt and all that you have seen. But hurry and bring my father down here.' Then he threw his arms around his brother Benjamin and wept on his shoulder. Joseph then kissed all his brothers and wept over them; and only then were his brothers able to talk with him." [33]

When John finishes the extended quote, he sits down. The others sit in stunned silence, not only because of the length of the quote that so freely flowed from his mouth but because of the truth it revealed.

Jesus claps his hands a second time that evening. "There is more to Joseph's story, but we don't have time to get into it tonight. Only think of this so you won't be too harsh with Jacob. None of the Archetypes of Blessings was without sin. Take some time to think about the sins in the lives of the others we have discussed: Noah, Abraham, and even Abel, whose sin was not recorded. Thinking about their sins will help you understand even more why Joseph is the perfect man to be called the Archetype of the Fifth Blessing."

---

[33] Gn 45: 1-15

CHAPTER 5

CONTEMPLATING THE FIRST

*When Jesus was born in **Bethlehem** of Judea, in the days of King Herod, behold, magi from the east arrived in Jerusalem, saying, 'Where is the newborn king of the Jews? We saw his star at its rising and have come to do him homage.' When King Herod heard this, he was greatly troubled, and all Jerusalem with him. Assembling all the chief priests and the scribes of the people, he inquired of them where the Messiah was to be born. They said to him, 'In **Bethlehem** of Judea, for thus it has been written through the prophet: 'And you, **Bethlehem**, land of Judah, are by no means least among the rulers of Judah; since from you shall come a ruler, who is to shepherd my people Israel.' Then Herod called the magi secretly and ascertained from them the time of the star's appearance. He sent them to **Bethlehem** and said, 'Go and search diligently for the child. When you have found him, bring me word, that I too may go and do him homage.* [34]

---

[34] " Mt 2:1-8, emphasis mine

Part One

Twilight circa AD 28: about five days after the fifth mountaintop experience on the northern shore of the Sea of Galilee

She had joined them when they passed through Nazareth before he fed the five thousand and after the locals rejected him, saying, "*Where did this man get such wisdom and mighty deeds.*" The locals had questioned everything about the family. "*Is he not the carpenter's son? Is not his mother named Mary and his brothers James, Joseph, Simon, and Judas? Are not his sisters all with us? Where did this man get all this? And they took offense at him. But Jesus said to them, A prophet is not without honor except in his native place and in his own house. And he did not work many mighty deeds there because of their lack of faith.*"[35]

Wishing to avoid controversies that draw attention to her, Mary left Bethlehem to join Jesus and the disciples. It would do her good to leave town for a while. Joseph had died, and even though Passover was several months away, she much preferred to travel the 100 or so kilometers to Jerusalem in the safety provided by the disciples. Her Son had told her they would take several mountainous detours, three to be exact, but she didn't mind.

She had missed his daily company. How does one tire of living with a man like him, a man so loving and wise, wanting to always serve instead of being served? She relished the time ahead. He,

---

[35] Mt 13:54-58

for His part, looked forward to the time with her. How does one tire of living with a woman like her, a woman so loving and wise, wanting to serve always instead of being served, at once so compassionate, whose eyes radiate holiness, whose heart radiates beauty, and whose words, few as they were, radiate perfect wisdom?

Besides, he knew how much she loved the old city, well, to be clear, the Temple in the city? She had once said the same thing about him, but it soon became clear that she and Joseph, for that matter, loved the Temple, too. While in the city, she might purchase a few items for the house from the local street vendors, but most of the time, she would be found in the Temple, not teaching the teachers as her Son had some twenty years ago, and certainly not conducting business with the money changers, but just sitting by herself quietly contemplating the religion of her youth and her Son.

She and Joseph, her husband, though simple, had learned to listen to and contemplate the Torah and the prophets every Sabbath in the synagogue with an eye toward their Son. Jesus, too, had taught them before he departed from home. In truth, she was a treasure chest of wisdom. Her wisdom found its strength and beauty as much in knowing God's will found in scripture and her beloved Son, Israel's Messiah, but so too from obeying God's will in every deed, word, and thought of her entire life. Imagine fifty or so years of sinless living; imagine what that had done for her. Despite her wisdom, she had never sought to be seen as wise. Rather, if asked anything by the curious rabbis of Nazareth, their hometown, she would direct them to her Son. *"Do whatever he tells you"* had become a familiar phrase heard from her lips. John had noted this.

To clarify, she and the other women joining her for the circuitous trip to Jerusalem were not idle stragglers. They would make themselves useful. They were happy to cook, clean, nurse wounds, and mend clothing. She did all of this while standing in the background. She avoided attracting any attention to herself. So silently had she traveled with them that even Matthew, perhaps the most observant among the Twelve, had not noticed her presence among them. Yes, meals had taken a fairly dramatic turn for the better, but he was too preoccupied with his blessings and archetype musings to give it much thought. He was content to enjoy the cooking without asking why it improved.

The Twelve first notice her precisely when she is actively trying to avoid being noticed. Jesus has just asked her to tell the story of His birth. She hadn't meant to raise her voice, but the request caught her off guard, and the sound of the surf suddenly ceased, causing her words to ring out much louder.

"What; you want me to stand before these men and speak. Son, women don't generally teach men in our culture. Worst of all, you want me to tell them about giving birth to you? Does a woman not deserve some degree of privacy?"

"Mother," Jesus says, dipping his toe in the cool water washing towards them in a gentle wave. "Yes, please share the birthing details and many other strange details of how I entered the world. Don't worry. I, the Lord, will be with you."

"I'm not sure I like when you use that line," she jokes. "Of course I will," she says as she looks into his eyes. "Don't I always do what you ask me to do," she continued with a wink, reminding him of her words at the Wedding feast of Cana.

He chuckles, and she hugs him. "Dear boy, what am I going to do with you?"

"Mother, you know from prior discussions, the better question to ask is; "What am I going to do without you?""

"Yes, my dear Son, but you've also told me you would always be with me, even if I can't see you, like I do now."

"Precisely, Mother, we will find time to talk about that as you watch me leave the world when I am raised up and put to death on a cross."

A painful pang surges through her heart. She heard Jesus say this before. She heard he said similarly concerning things to the disciples, that as the Messiah, he must suffer, be rejected, be killed, and rise again after three days. She had chosen to leave those comments unattended, but when she heard it directly from him, looked into his eyes, and saw his knowing look, she couldn't deny the truth. It was another reason to join him for this trek.

Brushing aside her ominous thoughts, she asks, "When, dear Son, do you want me to give this talk?"

"How about now, Mother? Twilight is upon us. The fire is fading. The air is cooling, and the crowd is gathering. Will you help me provide some warmth?"

"How did you know I would agree?"

"Do you really want me to answer that question?"

She smiles and steps towards an opening in the semicircular gathering that seems to open like a receding wave in front of her. She doesn't walk on water, but at times, water appears to accommodate her in special ways. Indeed, the tide moves out at her approach, the waves leave out a quick rustle, and the sea becomes completely calm. The moon looks down, bouncing a long trail of light across the water right to the water's edge and across the wet sand at her feet a short distance away.

John can't tell if it is the fire, the reflected moonlight, or perhaps some other light within her, but the light in her eyes and around her face looks positively angelic. As each person in the little gathering happens to glance her way, looks up, and beholds the woman standing before them, each one stops talking. Some even stop breathing. After everyone has joined the unified trance, and all is calm and bright, the Virgin Mother, with her Son at her side, opens her mouth. Matthew feels it, as do the others, a warm gust of air.

Part two

Twilight circa BC 4: In a small mountain village called Bethlehem in the land of Judea, the birthplace of Jesus Christ

The next instant, the group finds themselves in another time and place. No one knows how it happened, and no one dares ask. Their part is to be silent, observe, feel, and worship. Matthew watches and listens intently. He has positioned himself near the back, giving him a view of the small crowd before the Blessed Virgin and her Son. Are they angels or people? She is a person. He is a… person… and… God. She raises her hands as if preparing to speak but says nothing. A voice from heaven speaks. She looks up. Everyone looks up.

"Hail full of grace, the Lord is with you." [36]

---

[36] Lk 1:28b (Douay-Rheims Bible)

Matthew falls to his knees, prostrate, lowers his face to the ground, and kisses the wet, salty sand before him. He sees everyone else do the same. They are worshiping God, the source of all grace. Silence follows. She looks up towards the voice and the stars and moves her mouth. As she speaks, another warm gust blows over the group. It rustles up the sea. The noise of the wind and sea is suddenly deafening. They can see that she is conversing. She speaks and listens. After watching this conversation, they hear:

"Behold, I am the handmaid of the Lord. May it be done to me according to your word." [37]

After hearing her words, they follow her gaze up to a single star and a single beam of light that dances and sprinkles above her until its light fills the inside of her womb.

Matthew falls to his knees, prostrate, lowers his face to the ground, and kisses the wet, salty sand before him. He sees everyone else do the same. They are worshiping God, the giver of life. Silence follows. Is it a full nine minutes or nine months of silence? It is hard to tell. What follows next sounds like a mixture of words Matthew has read and others he has recently heard, one divine voice speaking to another divine voice. A third time, they look up and hear first, the ancient words.

"In the beginning, when God created the heavens and the earth — and the earth was without form or shape, with darkness over the abyss and a mighty wind sweeping over the waters—" [38]

They hear next the new words from the other divine voice. It says:

---

[37] Lk 1:38
[38] Gn 1:1-2

"You are the salt of the earth. But if salt loses its taste, with what can it be seasoned? It is no longer good for anything but to be thrown out and trampled underfoot." [39]

Matthew and the rest instinctively prostrate themselves and kiss the salty sand again. They are worshipping God, the creator. A fourth time, they look up and hear first, the ancient words.

"Let there be light, and there was light. God saw that the light was good. God then separated the light from the darkness. God called the light "day," and the darkness he called "night." Evening came, and morning followed- the first day." [40]

They hear, again, the new words from the other divine voice. It says:

"You are the light of the world." [41]

Matthew and the rest instinctively prostrate themselves and kiss the salty sand again. They are worshipping God, the source of all wisdom. A fifth time, they look up and hear first, the ancient words.

"God made the two great lights, the greater one to govern the day, and the lesser one to govern the night, and the stars. God set them in the dome of the sky, to illuminate the earth, to govern the day and the night, and to separate the light from the darkness. God saw that it was good. Evening came, and morning followed- the fourth day." [42]

They hear, again, the new words from the other divine voice. It says:

---

[39] Mt 5:13
[40] Gn 1:3-5
[41] Mt 5:14
[42] Gn 1:16-19

"You are the light of the world. A city set on a mountain cannot be hidden." [43]

Matthew and the rest instinctively prostrate themselves and kiss the salty sand again. They are worshipping God, the source of justice, rule, and order.

A sixth time, they look up and hear first, the ancient words.

"Then God said: Let us make human beings in our image, after our likeness. Let them have dominion over the fish of the sea, the birds of the air, the tame animals, all the wild animals, and all the creatures that crawl on the earth. God created mankind in his image; in the image of God he created them; male and female he created them." [44]

They hear, again, the new words from the other divine voice. It says:

"Nor do they light a lamp and then put it under a bushel basket; it is set on a lampstand, where it gives light to all in the house." [45]

Matthew and the rest instinctively prostrate themselves and kiss the salty sand again. They are worshipping God, the source of all beauty.

A seventh time, they look up and hear first, the ancient words.

"God looked at everything he had made, and found it very good. Evening came, and morning followed—the sixth day." [46]

They hear, again, the new words from the other divine voice. It says:

---

[43] Mt 5:14
[44] Gn 1:26-27
[45] Mt 5:15
[46] Gn 1:31

"Just so, your light must shine before others, that they may see your good deeds and glorify your heavenly Father." [47]

Matthew and the rest instinctively prostrate themselves and kiss the salty sand again, a seventh time. They are worshipping God, who is love. They kiss the salty sand a seventh time. After looking up to behold Jesus and His Mother, Mary, they kiss the salty sand a seventh time. And then they rest; God blesses them, and God loves them.

Part Three

Evening circa AD 28: about five days after the fifth mountaintop experience on the shore of the Sea of Galilee

As they raise their eyes an eighth time, the enchanted scene in front of them fades, but not entirely. They see Mary and Jesus again as they appeared at the start of the twilight, embracing each other, loving each other, a unified beam of light, a unified echo of wisdom, a sinless union of perfectly grace-filled persons. A long silence follows.

Thaddeus breaks the silence, "Lord, Did we just witness the first creation?"

Jesus answers, "Yes, Thaddeus, in a manner of speaking, you just witnessed the first creation."

Andrew asks, "Lord, Jesus, so we can say you were present at the first creation?"

---

[47] Mt 5:16

Jesus answers, "Yes, Andrew. I was present at the first creation."

Simon, the Zealot, asks, "Lord, Was your mother present at the first creation?"

Jesus answers, "No, Simon, she ushered in the New Creation when she said, *Behold, I am the handmaid of the Lord. May it be done to me according to your word.*"

Judas Iscariot missed most of the twilight meeting because he snuck away during the excitement. He had seized the opportunity to travel to the town with the money bags. Having snuck back in, he feigns a concerned voice and asks, "Were we here the whole time tonight? Should I count the money in the bags?"

Jesus answers: "No, you do not need to count the money. We were here the whole time. How about you, Judas? Struggling to think of an answer, Judas doesn't respond.

James, John's brother, asks, "Lord, did we see Adam and Eve?"

Jesus answers, "Yes, James. You saw them, for you looked with the eyes of faith."

James the Lesser, looking straight at Jesus and Mary, asks, "Am I seeing a second Adam and Eve before me now?"

Jesus answers, "Yes, James, you are looking at the second Adam and Eve."

Thaddeus, looking intently at Jesus and Mary, asks, "Am I looking at a Son and his Mother?"

Jesus answers, "Of course, Thaddeus, we stand before you."

Philip asks, "Lord, the deafening sound of the wind and sea; we heard it in the beginning; was that God speaking?"

Jesus answers: "Yes, Philip, how perceptive you have become. That was my Father speaking with his Daughter, my Mother. Every person born of a Woman has the potential to become a Child of

God. My Mother was made a Child of God at the moment of her conception, but make no mistake, I am not her Father. She is my Mother."

Nathaniel asks, "Lord, the beam of light filling the Woman, the warm gust of wind; we saw and heard them in the beginning; was that God speaking, also?"

Jesus answers, "Yes, Nathaniel. How perceptive you have become. God the Holy Spirit spoke and acted upon His Spouse, My Mother, for He is love."

During this entire dialogue, John remains silent. A series of thoughts flash through his mind, which he will share with the world later. He thinks, *"In the beginning was the Word, and the Word was with God, and the Word was God. He was in the beginning with God. All things came to be through him, and without him nothing came to be. What came to be through him was life, and this life was the light of the human race; the light shines in the darkness, and the darkness has not overcome it."* [48]

Jesus, reading his mind, says, "Yes, John, please share those thoughts when the time is right."

John, looking intently at Jesus and Mary, asks, "Lord, am I looking at a King and a Queen Mother?"

Jesus answers: "Yes, John, you are looking at a King and a Queen Mother, the Gebirah. The next time you see her, take a good look at her crown."

---

[48] Jn 1:1-5

Peter, sensing the solemnity of which he is a part, says, "Lord, it is good that we are here. If you wish, I will make two tents here, one for you and one for Mary."

Jesus answers, "I appreciate your good intentions, dear Peter, but that won't be necessary."

Matthew, who is waiting patiently for his turn, stands up and, bursting with joy, proclaims, "Peter, brothers, all, don't you see it? Don't you see the spiritual significance of what we watched then and are looking at now? Brothers, we are looking at the Archetype of the First Blessing."

A stunned silence follows, followed by "a has, and a general consensus of admiration for Matthew's wisdom, not to mention his advancing maturity and ability to remain focused, even when it requires a long spell of hearing others' thoughts. Then, everyone says, "Amen!"

Jesus answers: "All of you. What you just saw and see standing before you now is a second Adam and Eve, a Divine Son with His Mother, a Daughter of the Father. You just witnessed an embrace between a Divine Son and His Mother, the one and only God with humanity. You just witnessed a Groomsman, the King of Kings, and His Mother, the Queen of Queens, who will be crowned Queen Mother of Heaven when she is assumed into heaven. Indeed, you saw with your eyes, heard with your ears, and felt on your faces a warm compressed summary of a New Creation in the depths of your souls." An extended silence follows—the waves and wind, the creatures, all silent.

At length, Matthew speaks again, "Lord, if I am following this conversation correctly, it means that Adam and Eve are the Archetype of the First Blessing?"

Jesus answers, "Yes, Matthew, you are correct. They were the first humans to learn humility and model: *Blessed are the poor in spirit, for theirs is the kingdom of heaven.*"[49]

A loud chorus of asking and explaining voices follows. After a full ten minutes of animated conversation, Peter speaks. He asks a question all of them are asking.

"Lord, when did Adam and Eve model the First Blessing, before they sinned, or after?"

Jesus answers. "They modeled the First Blessing after sinning, Peter. Before sinning, Adam and Eve, humanity, having been made in the image and likeness of God, rested in heaven with their creator and Lord, God, Yahweh by name. At that time, all was a blessing. Let's follow the creation narrative to its conclusion on the seventh day. *Thus the heavens and the earth and all their array were completed. On the seventh day God completed the work he had been doing; he rested on the seventh day from all the work he had undertaken. God blessed the seventh day and made it holy, because on it he rested from all the work he had done in creation.*"[50]

Jesus continues. "In those days before sin entered the world, God was in all, and humanity was all in God. Blessing, or we can say 'Beatific' beauty and vision was the sum total of all reality and all creation. God's pervasive presence manifested Beatific beauty. Humanity's only experience was the Beatific vision, meaning what they felt, heard, and beheld with their eyes. There was no need for additional blessings. Nor could blessing be broken down into parts. The blessing of those days was one unified whole. God

---

[49] Mt 5:3
[50] Gn 2:1-3

had poured forth all blessings, and when He beheld the Man and the Woman made in His Image and likeness, he proclaimed it *very good*."

Peter dares to ask, "Please, Lord, can you clarify further?"

Jesus continues. "The telling word in that sentence is 'very.' God described everything he had created five times before, and each time, He described whatever he had created as merely 'good.' Think about that. He created the earth and the heavens, light, air, water, the sun and moon, mountains, seas, plants, fish, birds, and animals. He created in an instant that scientists will someday call the 'Big Bang' of creation, a massive momentous event. Nothing like that has happened since. A million lightning bolts compressed into one second wouldn't come close to creating a fraction of the power that went forth with that big bang. And yet, God describes this event and the days that followed five times as merely 'good.' Then, he created this Man and Woman, perhaps six feet tall. They don't look too unlike many of the other animals. At least many others had arms, legs, and faces. Yes, this couple comes, and God proclaims, *Very good*."[51]

Thoughts flash through Matthew's mind as he listens to Jesus. He asks a question. "Lord, you have described humanity's relationship with God before the fall with one word: Blessing. Can we discuss a verse that follows after humanity sinned?"

"Please, Matthew, recite the verse," answers Jesus.

---

[51] Gn 1:31

Matthew says, *"I will put enmity between you and the woman, and between your offspring and hers; They will strike at your head, while you strike at their heel."* [52]

Jesus smiles and says, "You have found the trail again, Matthew. You are heading up the right mountain. Recall that God had just cursed the devil disguised as a serpent. The curse on Satan was eternal separation from God, just what he wanted and asked for. After declaring the enmity that would follow between the Woman and her offspring and the devil, God made the man and his wife the Archetypes of the First Blessing. He immediately implemented plan B, the plan of nine Blessings, as it were."

"How, Lord," asks several disciples at the same time.

A long silence follows, and then a 'light bulb' lights up in Matthew's heart. "He made them the Archetypes of the First Blessing by giving them the means to learn humility. Poverty of spirit is another way to say humility."

John has the same 'light bulb' experience a moment later. "Think about it, brothers, while I quote the pertinent verses from Genesis. *To the woman he said: I will intensify your toil in childbearing; in pain you shall bring forth children. Yet your urge shall be for your husband, and he shall rule over you. To the man he said: because you listened to your wife and ate from the tree about which I commanded you, You shall not eat from it, Cursed is the ground because of you! In toil you shall eat its yield all the days of your life. Thorns and thistles it shall bear for you, and you shall eat the grass of the field. By the sweat of your brow you shall eat bread,*

---

[52] Gn 3:15

Until you return to the ground, from which you were taken; For you are dust, and to dust you shall return." [53]

Another long silence follows while everyone processes what Matthew said about the First Blessing's Archetype and what John quoted from Genesis.

Philip speaks, "I see it. The first blessing is *Blessed are the poor in spirit, for theirs is the kingdom of heaven.* By cursing the soil, God humbles men."

Nathaniel speaks next: "We can be sure, brothers, that the soil, the Garden called Eden, brought forth plenteous and sweet fruit, and working to obtain it was a concept that did not exist before the curse."

"But after the curse," continues Andrew, "after the curse, how difficult did it become for man to find sustenance? History reveals that humanity's journey back to God started with lessons in humility."

At this point, a new voice is heard. It is a woman's, Mary of Magdalene. She had also joined the group sometime after the fifth mountaintop experience. "Before any of the male folk here hazards to describe the curse placed on woman, let me tell you about that. I should know." She smiles at Mary, who smiles back and encourages her to proceed. "I will spare all of you the gory details of my experiences. Besides, some of you have delivered animals. Perhaps some of you have sat by and heard while a woman labored to deliver a child. Keep hold of those images, especially when you think badly about your wives or other women folk in your homes

---

[53] Gn 3:16-19

and towns. Suffice it to say, we have been bearing our share of the curse burden in nine-month increments since that fateful day in Eden."

Mary nods in agreement. She could identify with that. Mary Magdalene continues. "And, as if nine months of weight gain, tiredness, indigestion, and the like isn't enough, we are then made to bring forth the child through an opening ill-fitted, at least, size-wise, in my humble opinion."

Mary looks at her with deep sympathy. "Yes," Mary Magdalene continues, "it makes sense that our Lord has broken down the one blessing of heavenly bliss before sin into nine blessings after sin. It is a long and painful journey, but I, for one, am thankful. He has turned my mourning into dancing."

A very long silence follows as the men, especially, think hard. All have discovered a new appreciation for all women, especially their mothers. Many had seen women and infants die in childbirth and heard the agonizing screams, at times for days. They knew or heard of many women who had survived such an ordeal, only to deliver a stillborn and face lifelong complications of childbirth injury, paralysis of an extremity, and the inability to control one's urine or feces. Many of these women had become outcasts, forced to live like animals with the animals, the better to keep their stench away from the rest of the family.

Matthew had planned to say more, but after Mary Magdalene finished speaking and Mary, the Mother of Jesus, wrapped her arms around her, he sat down. They had summarized it well, far better than he could with words, no matter how inspired they may be. They had summarized it well. Everyone turns in for a good night's sleep except Matthew. He has thoughts that must be pondered before allowing himself to rest. He replays the first words of Mary's story. She started by reciting the eight sentences Matthew would write one day in a gospel describing Jesus's birth in Bethlehem. She repeated Bethlehem four times. Why? Was she drawing their attention to the fact that Bethlehem lay in the hill country of Judea? Was she calling them to consider that Bethlehem, only seven hundred and seventy-seven meters above sea level, was where Jesus's first mountaintop experience occurred? He liked that thought. It makes sense that His first mountaintop experience was modest and occurred on a humble mountain as if to emphasize the humility of the first blessing and the man who was born there.

CHAPTER 6

CONTEMPLATING THE SECOND

Then the devil took him up to a very high mountain, and showed him all the kingdoms of the world in their magnificence, and he said to him, "All these I shall give to you, if you will prostrate yourself and worship me." [54]

Midnight AD 28: about seven days after the fifth mountaintop experience, southeast of the Sea of Galilee in the desert heading towards the Decapolis

It is midnight, and Matthew is wide awake, wondering, "Why does he want to leave this place?" They had spent most of the last day and a half hiking southeast from the Sea of Galilee

---

[54] Mt 4: 8-9

towards the Decapolis. The journey provided time and space to contemplate and, frankly, to recuperate from that experience. Which experience? It was the one they had a few days back of Jesus' birth in Bethlehem in a way no one could have imagined possible. Even more thrilling, they had experienced the first days of creation, again, in a way that none of them could have imagined.

They sit in a cozy grove of date palms next to a swelling wadi trickling by. It must have rained not too long ago. He fills his leather pouch with cool water and joins the not-so-enthusiastic journeymen and women setting out at this late hour. They walk for more than an hour, guided by the lonely moon. They stop in the middle of the wilderness. Matthew wonders if Jesus has military plans for them at times like this. Who but the Roman Legions were made to endure such conditions as part of their training? At this dark hour, the desert life around them has been doing business for several hours. "More precisely," Matthew frets with a hint of trepidation, "those creatures of its realm that prefer darkness have been about their business."

He takes it all in. The rhythmic chirping of crickets provides a constant background melody. When all is quiet, they stand out. At times, they are joined by the buzz of cicadas and the high-pitched chirps of grasshoppers. An owl on the hunt provides a distinctive hoot. When other louder, larger animal noises intrude, the chirpers, buzzers, and hooters remain, providing the constant harmony of an eerie symphony. The haunting howls of coyotes echo across the barren landscape, lonely and mesmerizing and a stark reminder of the wild nature around them. Matthew shivers and thinks of David, the warrior trained as a shepherd fighting off lions and other wild killers to guard his sheep. He is sure David will be the Archetype of the Seventh Blessing, but they aren't here tonight to discuss that.

They gather in a small group without lighting a fire to hear Jesus tell the story of His second mountaintop experience. Matthew wants to believe that Jesus will protect them as David protected his sheep, should the occasion demand it. Still, the night feels mysterious, almost haunted. John does not miss it; he does not miss Jesus' plan to tell this second story in the dark in the middle of the wilderness. It will be another object lesson, filled with natural phenomena, ensuring the lesson sticks. Having shaken off his tiredness and fears, Matthew sits with the others waiting, eagerly anticipating the evening's events, the clean, chilly air rustling his mind to full attention.

Jesus and Mary are in front of them as they were when telling the story of the Archetype of the First Blessing. He hugs Mary, and she joins the group, sitting before him. He must tell this story alone. Jesus starts by reminding them that the Holy Spirit came upon him at his Baptism a day before the start of his forty days in the wilderness and led him to the desert to create this story alone until the very end.

"Now, close your eyes and follow along in your imagination the story I want to tell." Matthew takes a deep breath, closes his eyes, and follows the story carefully in his imagination.

In Matthew's imagination, they sit under a dark, starless sky. Jesus has gathered his disciples, the Twelve, Mary, and others around him. The air is thick with anticipation as Jesus opens his mouth to recount his harrowing experience in the desert. As if on cue, the desert symphony falls silent. Jesus is speaking. Matthew opens his eyes and notices that the same thing happened in reality.

Everything around them is silent except for his voice, calm yet powerful, painting vivid images of the barren wilderness where he had faced Satan, a vast, desolate, scorching hot desert.

"For forty days and nights, I wandered, fasting and praying. It was then that Satan came to me, seeking to exploit my hunger and weariness."

A hot breeze suddenly envelops the group. Matthew opens his eyes a second time, just long enough to see that they have not been teleported to another time or place. He closes his eyes again to imagine the scene.

Jesus is gaunt and weary, standing before a pile of stones. Satan, with a malicious smile, approaches him and says, *"If you are the Son of God, command these stones to become bread."* [55] Matthew feels the pangs of hunger that Jesus must have felt, a deep, gnawing emptiness in his own stomach.

Yet, he also senses Jesus' unwavering resolve as he replies, *"Man shall not live by bread alone, but by every word that comes from the mouth of God."* [56]

The scene shifts, and they are now on the pinnacle of the Temple in Jerusalem. The wind whips around them violently. Matthew peeks a third time. It is windy, but they are still sitting in the same desert on the same dark night. He closes his eyes and imagines Jesus, weak from the forty-day fast, staggering near the parapet's edge.

Satan challenges Him, *"If you are the Son of God, throw yourself down. For it is written, 'He will command his angels concerning you,*

---

[55] Mt 4:3
[56] Mt 4:4

and they will lift you up in their hands, so that you will not strike your foot against a stone.'" [57]

Matthew feels a rush of fear and doubt, the same emotions Satan sought to exploit. But he also feels the strength of Jesus' faith as he responds, *"It is also written: 'Do not put the Lord your God to the test.'"* [58]

The scene shifts again as Jesus describes a high mountain overlooking all the world's kingdoms. "So this is the second mountaintop experience of His life, Matthew thinks as he peeks, noticing that no one else is opening their eyes." Jesus' voice pulls him back to the imaginary, well, not so imaginary, scene.

"With a grand gesture, Satan offered me all the power and glory I could see, saying, *'All this I will give you if you bow down and worship me.'"* [59]

Matthew feels the allure of power and the weight of ambition, but then he hears Jesus' righteous indignation as He describes His response. *"Away from me, Satan! For it is written: 'Worship the Lord your God, and serve him only.'"* [60]

It is easier to count in some ways when one's eyes are closed, but Matthew opens his a fourth time. He is anxious and trying to distract himself. He thinks, "Three times, Satan had started his temptation with the words, *If you are the Son of God*. He mocked God, using his words from scripture and his words at Jesus'

---

[57] Mt 4:6
[58] Mt 4:7
[59] Mt 4:9b
[60] Mt 4:10

Baptism: *This is my beloved Son, with whom I am well pleased.* [61] Three times, Jesus rebuffed him with the words, '*It is written.*'"

Matthew suddenly notices that Jesus has stopped talking and is waiting until each of them opens their eyes and leaves the world of their vivid imaginations. As the last of the group opens their eyes, Jesus looks straight at Matthew and says, "Did you count them, Matthew? Has everyone opened their eyes," and then he winks at him. Matthew flushes, aware of his lack of faith but thankful for the Savior's patience.

With the visions of His second mountaintop experience fading, the disciples find themselves under the same dark, starless sky. The eerie symphony resumes, and their hearts pound with the intensity of what they have just imagined. Jesus waves his hand, and just as quickly, the symphony falls silent again. The disciples are in awe. They understand now, more than ever, the nature of the temptations they, too, will face: the hunger and thirst not for the satiation of physical needs but for spiritual needs, the desire for proof of God's love, the lure of worldly power, and last but not least, they understand the fear of death; all of these trials and others are not just a trial for Jesus but for all who follow him.

Jesus looks at each of them, his eyes filled with compassion and strength. "Remember," he says softly, "you are not alone in your struggles. As I overcame, so can you, with faith and steadfastness." The disciples nod, their resolve strengthened, ready to face their deserts with the courage and faith they had seen in their Master.

---

[61] Mt 3:17

Part Two

By now, the moon, having passed its culmination, sits about thirty degrees above the Western horizon, casting a gentle golden glow. The glow is interrupted in places where it passes through a grey blanket of Stratus clouds to create a mosaic of shadows and highlights on the ground in front of them. Jesus continues to look around at the group, asking the question everyone has on their mind in His very silence. The long silence continues.

Matthew senses that everyone is waiting for him to speak, so he breaks the silence, his voice thoughtful. "Jesus' temptations reminded me of the story of Abel and Cain. In a way, Abel embodies the Second Blessing: *Blessed are they who mourn, for they will be comforted.*"[62]

John nods, his eyes reflecting the moonlight. "Abel's offering was genuine, a true act of repentance and devotion. He mourned his sins and sought God's favor with a sincere heart. Unlike Cain, who gave in to the temptation to fake his repentance."

James leans forward, his brow furrowed in contemplation. "Cain's offering was more about appearance than substance. He wanted to seem repentant without truly feeling it. When God rejected his offering, instead of mourning his sin and seeking true repentance, he gave in to anger and jealousy."

Andrew adds, "Abel's mourning was not just about feeling sorrowful. It was about recognizing his need for God's grace and mercy. He overcame the temptation to present a false front, to

---

[62] Mt 5:4

pretend he was something he was not. His mourning was genuine, and he found comfort in God's acceptance."

Even while the comments by these disciples reveal that Jesus' lesson has stuck, Thomas, always the skeptic, asks, "But why is mourning so important? Why does it bring comfort?"

Peter replies, "Mourning our sins brings us closer to God. It is an acknowledgment of our need for His forgiveness and a step toward true repentance. Abel's genuine mourning showed his humility and dependence on God, which is why he was comforted and accepted."

Matthew speaks again, his voice filled with conviction. "Abel is the Archetype of the Second Blessing." He is a reminder that we, too, will face temptations to take the easy way out, to fake our repentance or devotion. But true comfort and acceptance come from genuine mourning and humility." The disciples fall silent, each lost in their thoughts. The night seems to hold its breath as if listening to their reflections and awaiting Jesus' response.

Jesus motions toward Mary, and she joins him in front of the others. Under the same dark, starless sky, Jesus and Mary stand before the disciples, their presence serene yet filled with a profound sense of purpose. They are the second Adam and Eve, bearing the weight of humanity's struggles and hopes. The disciples watch in silence, sensing the gravity of the moment.

Jesus begins to speak, his voice carrying the sorrow of ages. "Mary, do you remember my stories about the pain of Abel's death? The salty bitterness of his blood, the sorrow of his loss?" Mary nods, her eyes glistening with unshed tears. Jesus turns to the disciples, his gaze intense and filled with love. "Abel's death was not just a loss; it is a lesson, a lesson about the dangers of giving in to temptation, of letting pride and anger rule our hearts. Cain and Abel were confronted with a choice, and their responses shaped their destinies."

Mary steps closer to Jesus. She doesn't say anything, but it is evident that she is reminding him to say something else. Jesus speaks. "Her heart aches for you, her children. You will face similar challenges and temptations that will test your faith and resolve."

John thinks, "Her presence always emphasizes the maternal love of a mother for her children."

Jesus continues, "Cain gave in to his darker impulses, while Abel sought to remain true to God. It is not enough to simply avoid sin; you must actively seek righteousness. You must mourn your sins genuinely, as Abel did, and find comfort in God's grace."

Mary looks at Jesus again, pleading just by looking at him for him to continue. Jesus continues. "You must support each other, just as we support you. Lean on one another in times of weakness. Lean on her, and she will always lead you to me. Remember that true strength comes from humility and faith."

The disciples listen intently, their hearts heavy with the weight of the message. They understand their journey will be difficult but also feel a renewed sense of purpose. They are determined to honor Abel's lessons and overcome the challenges ahead. They will rely on each other and the two who stand before them. Jesus and Mary look at each other, a silent understanding passing between them. They have relived the pain of Abel's death and tasted the salty bitterness of his blood, and now they stand united in their hope for the disciples. Jesus calls them brothers. Mary knows her children can overcome the trials that await them with faith, hope, love, and support.

Jesus looks at Matthew and says, "You are moving in the right direction, my dear tax collector. Abel is the Archetype of the Second Blessing, the first brother to die for and honor the first Adam and Eve and the first child of God to die for and worship God, my Father, with his life."

Matthew smiles, even blushes. It feels good to be affirmed by the teacher so candidly in front of the others. Is the group moving towards completely accepting this one-time tax collector and thief? Might the side jokes and murmurings stop? Besides, he thinks prayerful contemplation is a good practice. He looks again at Jesus and recalls how he has worked like a master builder to build cohesion among his disciples while not dampening their individuality. Each has strengths to offer. He wants that individuality to manifest, especially in their approach to scripture. Each comes to the Word of God from a unique experience God intends to use. It hardly made sense to bicker over the very attributes that will make them strong as a unified group.

Jesus then asks a series of questions designed to encourage creative contemplation. "Have I ever said that you should stop looking for other characters in the Torah who manifest these blessings simply because we have focused on one in whom they seem to shine the brightest? Have I ever said that an Archetype must always be just one person? Might it be possible that an Archetype could be two people, namely a couple? Did you not see this with Adam and Eve? Could it be possible that an Archetype could be many people, like perhaps this group, the entire nation of Israel, or perhaps the body of believers who would come to know and love me through your collective witness?"

There is a general stirring when he says, 'your witness,' for the two-word phrase He used can also be understood as 'your martyrdom.' Before anyone has too much time to speculate about this, Jesus continues. "I am not asking anyone to answer these questions now. File them. Catalog them, as dear Matthew certainly has already for future contemplation." Matthew blushes again. "Now, let's consider Abel more deeply," says Jesus.

Matthew and John react almost simultaneously at the mention of a deepening discussion of Abel. They are anxious to share ideas that rush to the surface from deep prior contemplation about him being the Archetype of the Second Blessing. Because he is younger and generally modest, not to mention Jesus' affirmations of Matthew, John sweeps his hand in a wide circle towards Matthew and says with a smile, "The floor is yours, my kindred contemplative spirit." Matthew reciprocates, charming the others, "Youth before beauty, my young-un," as he sweeps an even wider circle towards John.

John stands up, and after the good-natured banter subsides, he speaks. "It is true, brothers, that the scriptures say very little about Abel. Interestingly, Abel is named seven times in Genesis."

"Aha," Matthew muses, "I hadn't bothered to count that. I need to consult with you more often."

"Perhaps there is something to seven in this," John responds, "but I mention it to draw a contrast with Cain, his murderer, who is named eighteen times. Furthermore, Genesis offers no words from Abel. We learn about him only through his actions. In contrast, we read a candid conversation between God and Cain. Thus, even though Genesis allows us to learn about Abel only through his actions, we can learn much about him by contemplating the contrasting images between the silent martyr and the outspoken murderer." John pauses and then continues.

"We know they were both sons of Adam and Eve. Therefore, both had inherited a sinful nature. Both, in the course of their lives, would have learned by word and example what righteous and unrighteous living entailed. Both would have given their parents and each other, not to mention God, reasons for disappointment. Both would have acted unrighteously at some point. We can deduce with absolute certainty that both acted unrighteously, at least once; why? Because they made sacrifices for God. As we have already heard, whatever the two sons had done wasn't as important as their attitude after realizing the error and sinfulness of their actions. We see it in God's reaction to their sacrifices.

The LORD looked with favor on Abel and his offering, but on Cain and his offering he did not look with favor.

Cain's reaction to God's reactions gives us still further insight into his heart. *So Cain was very angry and dejected.*

It is noteworthy that God did not reject Cain. *Then the LORD said to Cain: Why are you angry? Why are you dejected? If you act rightly, you will be accepted; but if not, sin lies in wait at the door: its urge is for you, yet you can rule over it.*

God wasn't pleased with Cain's gift, but rather than rejecting him, God offered a remedy for correcting his confession. Genesis tells us what happened next.

Cain said to his brother Abel, 'Let us go out in the field.' When they were in the field, Cain attacked his brother Abel and killed him." [63]

---

[63] Gn 4:4b-8

John pauses for effect, to let the moment's import settle on them. At that moment, an owl soars above them, its wings slicing through the air; with a piercing screech, it announces its presence. Its keen eyes, catching every glint of moonlight, scan the desert below, searching for the quick movement of small prey. The owl's cry is a testament to hunger and a declaration of impending death.

John resumes his reflections. "We all understand the importance of having a penitential attitude when confessing sins. One should feel sorry for one's wrongdoings. If one doesn't feel sorry, one should not ask God for forgiveness, or at the very least, ask God to grant a penitential spirit. Help me, Lord, to understand the gravity of my sin and to feel sorry for it, one might pray. What happened to Cain and Abel foreshadowed what has happened to humanity ever since. Everyone will sin. Some will repent, while others will harden their resolve against God. Some will mourn and receive the blessing of comfort from God, and others will not. Let me repeat the second blessing: *Blessed are they who mourn, for they will be comforted.*"

John stops. A palpable silence follows. It is as if John has lifted everyone's eyes and hearts to a new level. Jesus smiles broadly. Matthew looks at John with surprise, fascination, and admiration.

"But wait," John says. "There's more. Do you recall the first words Jesus said after the Nine Blessings?"

"Yes," Andrew answers. "He said, *You are the salt of the earth.*"[64]

"Correct," says John. "Indeed, Abel was the first to salt the earth. See how Genesis conveys this idea in God's words to Cain.

---

[64] Mt 5:13a

God then said: What have you done? Your brother's blood cries out to me from the ground! [65] We all know, brothers, from experience that blood has a salty taste. [66] I find it fascinating that Jesus's words in the Sermon on the Mount immediately after the ninth blessing warn about human saltiness. *But if salt loses its taste, with what can it be seasoned? It is no longer good for anything but to be thrown out and trampled underfoot."* [67]

John stops again, giving the others time to catch up. Matthew thinks, "He leaps effortlessly from one spiritual truth to the next. I need to spend more time with him."

John continues. "See how God applied these words to Cain. *Now you are banned from the ground that opened its mouth to receive your brother's blood from your hand. If you till the ground, it shall no longer give you its produce. You shall become a constant wanderer on the earth.* [68] Thus, we see Jesus summarizing the fate of humanity by pointing us back to the first two brothers. Those who manifest the first blessing, being poor in spirit before God, the second blessing, mourning their sin, and the third, meekly depending on God, will salt the earth with their blood; they will and inherit the earth and find Sabbath rest, while those who do not will wander restlessly for eternity."

"Bravo," Jesus says while applauding. "We don't have time to pursue the gigantic spiritual leap that John has just taken. Just

---

[65] Gn 4:10
[66] The average 70-kilogram person has about five liters of blood filled with sodium and potassium chloride salts, so Abel was the first to salt the earth.
[67] Mt 5:13b
[68] Gn 4:11-12

realize that in quoting from the Sermon on the Mount, the first words following the Nine Blessings, he has illustrated a pattern of investigating, interpreting, and understanding the Nine Blessings, meaning that one should examine the rest of the words in the Sermon on the Mount first to understand what they mean. We have been relating them to these archetypes, and this exercise has taken us far afield to the first books in the Torah. However, you must also return to the Sermon on the Mount to understand the Nine Blessings."

"Wow, just wow," says Peter. The others, all except Matthew, express a similar sentiment. Matthew's head is aching with the thought that Jesus has just opened a new massive treasure chest of words to explore. Doing some quick math and using numbers he had determined from a prior mental exercise, he murmurs to himself. "His Sermon on the Mount contained two thousand two hundred thirty-nine words, and the Nine Blessings comprise the first one hundred twenty words. That means there are two thousand one hundred-nineteen words to consider when trying to understand how Jesus explains the Nine Blessings. It is too much. Lord, what would you have me do?" He looks around. Everyone else has fallen asleep. "Lord, what would you have me do," he repeats. Eventually, he closes his heavy eyelids and succumbs to a heavenly and well-needed sleep.

CHAPTER 7

CONTEMPLATING THE SEVENTH

When they drew near Jerusalem and came to Bethphage on the Mount of Olives, Jesus sent two disciples, saying to them, "Go into the village opposite you, and immediately you will find an ass tethered, and a colt with her. Untie them and bring them here to me." [69]

Part One

Spring, AD 30: sunset, the close of Yom Shabbat, the seventh day and start of Yom Rishon, the first day, a journey from the city of Jericho, 275 meters below sea level, to the Mount of Olives near Bethphage and Bethany, approximately 825 meters above sea level

---

[69] Mt 21:1-2

Matthew makes the calculations. Considered from the perspective of distance, the journey from Jericho to the Mount of Olives in Bethage and nearby Jerusalem is about thirty kilometers. They will complete it in one day—no problem for the hardy and well-conditioned disciples who had spent the last three years hiking from town to town and mountaintop to mountaintop. Besides, they were well-fed at the house of Zacchaeus, another tax collector who had become a follower of Jesus.

Considered from the perspective of altitude to be climbed, starting at the low point in the valley in which Jericho lies to the high point, the Mount of Olives and Jerusalem, they will ascend approximately 1100 meters or about six stadia.

Considered from the perspective of duration, that is, from today until Passover, their temporal destination and endpoint, the seventh mountaintop experience will cover six days.

The time spent hiking for John and Matthew is nearly synonymous with time spent contemplating. For the other disciples, it is synonymous with time spent conversing. To their credit, the conversations are often deep and relevant to the spiritual journey Jesus is leading them on. Jesus, for His part, spends time doing both, at times wandering along quietly, praying to his Father, and at other times, engaging the conversationalist, probing them with questions, uncovering truths, bringing concepts and ideas together when everyone else is lost. And still, other times, he pulls the two contemplatives back to earth and, just as often, catapults them back into the heavens.

Matthew's contemplations on this day are troubling. They center around Jesus' genealogy, which he plans to include in his account. He knows it should follow his father Joseph's lineage.

He considers the idea of mentioning four women, each of whom would cause the self-righteous, hypocritical Pharisees to pause before scandalizing Mary: Tamar, whom her father-in-law Judah impregnated; [70] Rahab, a Canaanite prostitute whom Salman impregnated; [71] Ruth, a widowed Moabite woman, meaning her lineage started with the incestuous union of Lot and his oldest daughter, [72] and Bathsheba, the wife of Uria, who David had placed on the front line of battle, leading to his death and paving the way for him to pursue Bathsheba, who he had previously impregnated through an adulterous union. [73] Let them consider these stories and these men and women before they condemn her and him. However, even as he envisions shutting the hypocrites up, he's not sure if portraying the Holy Family lineage in such a scandalous manner is a good idea. Everyone who knew Joseph and who knows Mary and Jesus see plainly their holiness and righteousness. The exceptions are the Pharisees and other hypocrites. Joseph was an exceptionally righteous man. Devoted to Mary and sharing with her a vow of celibacy in their prenuptial agreement, he devoted himself fully to serving her, Jesus, and God. He was the model husband, father, and man of God that all men should strive to emulate.

Alongside this 'scandalous' question, Matthew has been struggling with another more practical question. If he includes Jesus' genealogy in his written summary of his time with Jesus,

---

[70] Gn 38
[71] Mt 1:5
[72] Gn 19:30-38
[73] 2 Sm Chapters 11 and 12

he wants to get it right, to name the right men and the right number of men who preceded Him. And yet, the genealogies are not consistent. He has examined several genealogies in the Torah, including those in Genesis, Ruth, 1 Chronicles, and 2 Samuel. "Why can't things be clear and consistent, especially as simple as a genealogy? One man fathers a son, and that son fathers a son, and so on." - this bothered him. It also bothered him that it bothered him. "Others seem to glide right past apparent discrepancies. Why do I always get stuck in these thorny questions." After considerable deliberation, Matthew thinks portraying it as forty-one or forty-two men makes the most sense, although he can't decide which.

About halfway through the thirty-kilometer trek, Jesus warns the disciples that things will be speeding up. By this, he means there will be many momentous events and conversations they will want to discuss but will not have the time to do so. He reminds them again, especially Matthew, that the Holy Spirit will bring those things needed for their future ministries and writing to their minds.

Matthew tries to stay calm, but he fails miserably. Jesus keeps reminding them of Jerusalem and how He *"must go to Jerusalem and suffer greatly from the elders, the chief priests, and the scribes, and be killed and on the third day be raised."* [74] The more Jesus talks like this, the more Matthew perseverates on details that don't seem to matter. What is Jesus talking about, and how will he, Matthew, ever get it all written down? Matthew struggles to keep pace mentally with the rapidly unfolding events of this week of

---

[74] Mt 16:21

preparation for Passover more than to maintain the pace of travel from Jericho to the Mount of Olives and Jerusalem. He barely succeeds at the second and fails miserably at the first. It is an unwise endeavor and could even be considered foolish. The Lord has told him not to worry. It is a time to live in the present with the people before you, not in your head ruminating about those who have passed by.

Even as he scolds himself once again for obsessing, he lapses back into his world of questions—it is one of the ways Matthew copes with growing anxiety, especially when occupying his mind with number games or number associations. Perhaps this trait is a residue from his tax-collecting days.

Matthew recalls Jericho, the city of sevens, because that was the number of days God instructed Israel's priests to march around the city with the Ark of the Covenant in front. He had instructed them,

"Have all the soldiers circle the city, marching once around it. Do this for six days, with seven priests carrying ram's horns ahead of the ark. On the seventh day, march around the city seven times, and have the priests blow the horns." [75]

"How could any synagogue-attending Jew hear that story and not think of the Genesis creation story? God made the world in six days but did not consider the work complete until he had established the seventh day as a day of rest.

Why did God say 'the seventh day' three times in the Genesis account?" It is a question that has lingered in his thoughts for a

---

[75] Jos 6:2-5

long time, but he has to let it go, as hard as that is, because many other seven associations are rushing into his mind.

His mind is drawn back to Jesus' genealogy. "What if he were to portray it as three groups of fourteen? In this case, one could also think of it as six groups of seven. With Jesus' arrival at the end of the sixth seven, should the world consider that it was entering the time of the seventh seven? There were twelve baskets left over after He fed five thousand. Why were there seven left over after He fed four thousand? Jesus himself had asked them to consider that question.

There was another big number-related question. Did the sixth mountaintop experience occur after six days or eight days? They debated the question, and Jesus did not provide an answer when asked about it. If it occurred after six days, that means the Transfiguration occurred on the seventh day, after the first time Jesus shared the plan that He must die? Did Jesus plan for that sixth mountaintop experience to occur six days after He rebuked Peter and said to him, *Get behind me, Satan! You are an obstacle to me. You are thinking not as God does, but as human beings do.* [76] Is six Satan's number? Is seven God's number?

But what if the sixth mountaintop experience occurred after the eighth day? What does that mean?" His gut told him repeatedly that the ninth mountaintop experience and meeting the Archetype of the Ninth Blessing would be a blessing of incalculable proportion. He had originally surmised that Jesus must be the Archetype of the Ninth Blessing, but after the enchanted evening by the sea,

---

[76] Mt 16:23

he figured it to be Jesus and Mary, His Mother. Matthew's brain ached as the questions continued, yet he could not stop asking them. Nor could he stop trying to answer them.

"Was Peter also fixated on numbers? Why did he ask Jesus, not too many days later, when they were in Capernaum, *Lord, if my brother sins against me, how often must I forgive him? As many as seven times?"* [77]

Yes, Matthew recalled, that question followed Jesus' instructions on the importance of forgiveness, and then came the shocking statement: *"Whatever you bind on earth shall be bound in heaven; and whatever you loose on earth shall be loosed in heaven."* [78]

He could hardly think about the implications of that statement. Still, why had Peter, of all people, asked the number question?" It caused his stomach to flutter, but then there was the Lord's response: *"I say to you, not seven times but seventy-seven times."* [79]

"Ok, that settles it," Matthew thinks. "Jesus thinks the number seven has special significance." That thought sends a thrill through his spine. "Maybe," he thinks, "I am not so crazy after all." Then he thinks again: "Had Jesus said seventy-seven times, or seventy times seven?" He scolds himself again- "Why do I find little unimportant questions to dwell on?"

Then, it dawns on him that it is an important question because seventy times seven equals four hundred ninety. "Again, any Sabbath-observing Jew should immediately think of Daniel's prophecy of the 'seventy weeks.' A week is seven days. Did he mean

---

[77] Mt 18:21
[78] Mt 16:19
[79] Mt 18:22

by seven weeks, seven years, and was he drawing attention to an event that would occur four hundred ninety years later? It could hardly be a coincidence that Jesus arrived about four hundred ninety years after Daniel prophesized that *the abomination that causes desolation' would occur.*"[80] He suddenly stops the self-chatter, frozen, fretting, worrying. "What is happening? Where are we headed? What is the real reason for our journey to Jerusalem?" He shutters when he thinks like this. Today, he shutters so hard that his entire body shakes involuntarily.

Part Two

Later on Yom Rishon, Palm Sunday, the first day, an evening on the Mount of Olives near Bethphage and Bethany

Suddenly, the air is filled with happy voices. They have arrived at the day's destination, Bethany, without Matthew even noticing. Mary, Martha, and Lazarus, whom he had raised from the dead, run out of their house and hug Jesus and the others, tripping over each other happily, chattering continuously.

"Mary, show them where to wash up," says Martha. Mary lingers with Jesus, lovingly engaging Him in conversation while Lazarus watches, smiling.

"Come on in and sit down," Martha says, breaking up the conversation. You must be hungry. We have plenty for everyone."

---

[80] Dn 9:27, 11:31, 12:11

"Spending the evening in Bethany with these friends will do them good," Matthew thinks.

Jesus knows Matthew's thoughts and thinks, "Little does he know the significant roles they will play. Martha will ensure we are well-fed, washed, and ready for tomorrow's big day. Mary will do her part, ensuring I am prepared, anointing my head and feet with expensive nard and wiping them with her hair. When Judas gripes about 'wasting' the nard, I will inform him she is preparing me for burial, and the room will become silent."

The following morning, Matthew and John are the first ones up. They go outside and sit in a grove of trees. They are deep in conversation and don't notice when the group heads out. Matthew shares his troubling thoughts from the previous day.

"Everyone understands the significance of Jerusalem," Matthew says to John. "Its' history is related in some manner to many of the most significant events in God's dealings with His people. Melchizedek, King of Righteousness and King of Salem, satisfied Abraham's righteousness with bread and wine. Thirty-five to forty years later, or perhaps a biblical generation, Abraham went to the same mountain to sacrifice his beloved son Isaac. After God stopped him and provided the lamb for the sacrifice, Abraham named the place *Yahweh-yireh*, or Jerusalem, which means, *On the mountain the LORD will provide.*"[81]

They pause to reflect. John speaks. "Approximately one thousand years later, David surely understood the significance of this place, for soon after his ascendency to the throne, he marched

---

[81] Gn 22:14

up there, seized the city for Israel, and planned to build a house for God. David never had the opportunity to build that house, but 2 Chronicles tells us that Mount Moriah was where Solomon built the Temple in Jerusalem." [82]

Without missing a beat, Matthew continues. "Consider, too, what David wrote in the Psalms; rest assured, he saw the thread of covenantal meals between God and His people and how they occurred on mountains. *You water the mountains from your chambers; from the fruit of your labor the earth abounds. You make the grass grow for the cattle and plants for people's work to bring forth food from the earth, wine to gladden their hearts, oil to make their faces shine, and bread to sustain the human heart.*" [83]

"And now," John continues, "approximately one thousand years later, Jesus, the Messiah, is marching towards that same mountainous city. I fear another battle that does not bode well for him. Recall, He told us he will be killed."

Matthew answers, "Right, John. He says we must go there for the Passover feast, but the way He has been talking, I am not sure what kind of feast He has planned. Ironically, it appears that His own people, the Jewish leaders, will be the ones leading the charge to have Him killed." With this foreboding thought pressing in on them, they stop talking. Martha approaches and informs them that the others left for Jerusalem about five minutes ago. They jump up and trot to catch them.

Matthew picks up right where they left off. "It makes perfect sense that Jesus' own people are the ones leading the charge to

---

[82] 2 Ch 3:1
[83] Ps 104:13-15

kill him- this is why David is uniquely qualified to be named the Archetype of the Seventh Blessing; *Blessed are the peacemakers, for they shall be called children of God.* [84]

I realize it is hard to envision David as a peacemaker in light of his well-known military career. David was a warrior for most of his adult life. However, David's worst wars were not with enemies outside of Israel. His worst enemies came from within Israel and even from within his immediate family. Only by looking at these wars can we understand David's peacemaking qualities and see how he, in particular, is uniquely qualified to be called the Archetype of the Seventh Blessing." As Matthew completes the story, there is silence between them, both taking and giving the other ample time to contemplate.

The two contemplatives suddenly stop and stoop on their haunches to observe wildlife. It is a long line of black ants trooping across the path they are walking on. The other disciples have hurried past, but the two contemplatives stop and watch, sharing a fascination with nature. They watch the line of ants extending at least one hundred feet into the trees until reaching a massive hollowed-out standing tree trunk. Matthew points to another line of red ants hurrying to the same trunk from another direction.

"You know they are warring. I can see it from here. Why do you suppose they can't learn to get along? The only difference between these two families of insects is the color of their bodies. They are brothers. They are family on some level, and still, they

---

[84] Mt 5:5

will kill each other over one trunk when there are so many more to be had."

John appreciates the natural illustration of his point and continues. "David's first civil war was against the house of Saul, Israel's first king. David did not want to fight Saul. It was Saul who, out of jealousy and fear, waged war against David. Saul pursued David, making him an outcast in his own land. Ironically, David had to seek refuge in Philistine, the first of Israel's enemies he defeated. He was reduced to pretending to be insane and eventually found refuge in a cave near the town of Adullam. Think of it. David fights Saul's battles and wins him fame and wealth. How did Saul show gratitude? He tried to kill David twelve times, at least, according to the biblical texts. And what was David's response to all of this? David spared Saul's life, not once, but twice. It's all there in the book of 1 Samuel."

They see they are falling behind the others, stand up, and stop watching the ants. After a brisk forty-leg jog to catch up, John resumes the story. "David was not motivated to spare Saul's life by cool calculating political maneuvering. He loved Saul. Consider his reaction when learning of Saul and his son Jonathan's deaths if you doubt this. *David seized his garments and tore them, and so did all the men with him. They mourned and wept and fasted until evening for Saul and his son Jonathan, and for the people of the LORD and the house of Israel, because they had fallen by the sword.* [85]

---

[85] 2 Sm 1:11-12

Consider too the long lament David wrote to honor Saul and his son Jonathan, also found in 2 Samuel a few verses later. David's words do not reflect a man satisfied with revenge. They do not reflect a victor gloating over his defeated enemy. Rather, they reflect a man who loved his enemy and did everything he could to maintain a peaceful relationship with him."

Matthew picks up the historical review. "Other notable wars David fought with his kinsmen included Shimei, a member of the house of Saul, who cursed David during his flight from Absalom. There was also Sheba, son of Bichri, who led a rebellion against David after Absalom's death. David's military commander Joab also turned against him by supporting Adonijah's claim to the throne instead of Solomon, whom David had chosen as his successor. These wars are described in 2 Samuel and 1 Kings."

John says, "We should not leave our considerations of David's peacemaking wars without looking closer at the story of his son Absolom, the third son of King David and Maacah. 2 Samuel provides a lengthy and clear account of Absolom's treachery, his vile attempts to wrest the kingdom from his father, David. Deceit, plots, political and public harem-stealing- by all of this and more did Absolom provoke David.

David had to flee Jerusalem as Absolom moved in to take power." Suddenly, another thought seizes him, which he shares in earnest. "It was from the Mount of Olives that David found himself with his small band of followers watching Absolom and his army take control of Jerusalem. Recall how David grieved. Let me quote it for you. *As David went up the ascent of the Mount of Olives, he wept without ceasing. His head was covered, and he was walking barefoot. All those who were with him also had their heads covered and were weeping as they went."* [86]

That had to be the low point of David's reign," laments Matthew. "Will it, meaning the Mount of Olives, be the low point of Jesus' reign? Did you notice how 2 Samuel specifies the Mount of Olive three times?" [87]

John continues after a pause without answering the question. "Despite what Absolom had done, David grieved his death. Recall how David responded when he heard the news.

The king was shaken, and went up to the room over the city gate and wept. He said as he wept, 'My son Absalom! My son, my son Absalom! If only I had died instead of you, Absalom, my son, my son!" [88]

"John," Matthew says, "we have contemplated the first part of the seventh blessing, *Blessed are the peacemakers,* to see how it finds clear fulfillment in David. Now, we must consider the scriptures that explicitly link David to the second part of the seventh blessing- this idea is expressed clearly in Nathan's oracle to David, found earlier in 2 Samuel. Recall what David said after taking residence in his house in Jerusalem after the Lord *Had given him rest from his enemies on every side.* [89] After fighting many wars, David finally enjoyed a time of peace with Israel's enemies."

Suddenly, John stops and puts his hand to his ear. Matthew does the same. They hear the high-pitched tweets of sparrow fledglings. Looking to their right, they spot the nest as the mother

---

[86] 2 Sm 15:13
[87] 2 Sm 15:17, 23, and 30
[88] 2 Sm 19:1
[89] 2 Sm 7:1

sparrow brings them something to eat. John silently puts up two fingers and points to another nest in the same tree. They watch the same scene there.

Matthew continues with a smile and a whisper. "Given his peaceful situation, David told Nathan he wanted to build a house for God. Of course, he was talking about a temple which, we have seen, would be built by his son, Solomon. God responded to this request by flipping everything around. David wouldn't build God a house. God would build David's house, meaning David's dynasty, and this Davidic dynasty would last forever." [90]

Still whispering but with more earnestness, Matthew continues, "Recall a key phrase from Nathan's oracle. *I will be a father to him, and he shall be a son to me.*" [91]

"*I will be a father to him, and he shall be a son to me,*" repeats John, ending the hushed speech. "If I may summarize," he continues loudly, "We can see in the Sermon He was preaching how Jesus advanced the call of the Seventh Blessing. At first, with the seventh blessing, he said, Peacemakers *will be called children* [92] of God. But later, after one has demonstrated true peacemaking by loving their enemies, He says, That you *may be children* [93] of God the Father. Those who will be *called, become* God's children if they are true peacemakers. They move from being **called** children of God to **being** children of God the Father, if they *love their enemies*. They move from theoretical to actual intimacy with God as their Father."

---

[90] 2 Sm 7:2-16
[91] 2 Sm 7:14
[92] Mt 5:9
[93] Mt 5:43-44

Part Three

Sunrise, Palm Sunday, the first day – entering Jerusalem, 2500 feet above sea level

They are hiking very quickly toward Jerusalem. Jesus has set out at a breakneck speed, eyes dead ahead, neither looking right nor left, not conversing, pushing them all to keep up the pace. Matthew looks at the sun's height above the horizon and estimates they covered the three kilometers in less than half an hour. As they reach the outskirts of Jerusalem, Matthew and John are jolted out of a deep conversation by a wildly cheering crowd. They look about forty meters ahead and see Jesus riding on a donkey. They run to catch them. Peter, James, and others struggle to clear the way to protect Jesus from the enthusiastic crowd pressing in on them. Fortunately, many in the crowd help clear the way by placing palm branches on the road before him. Many of them shout, *"Hosanna to the Son of David; blessed is he who comes in the name of the Lord; hosanna in the highest."* [94]

The popularity Jesus enjoyed during His first entry into Jerusalem seems to confirm that they are amidst an ever-improving seventh mountaintop experience. Still, Matthew recalls David's story. His anxiety drives Matthew to attempt to catalog the events, even during this commotion. Did He say he would be "mocked and scourged and crucified?"

---

[94] Mt 21:9

Matthew notes one other salient fact, which he feels certain the others missed. However, he who pays attention to such facts, even if obsessively, didn't miss it. They were descending. Literally speaking, the Mount of Olives in Bethphage was the high point of this day. Would it become the low point of another day, he asked himself again? So, while many cheered as they moved down into Jerusalem, Matthew did not. He has seen how easily a fickle crowd could be moved from adulation to a frenzied and angry mob. He recalls that, over the past few days, Jesus has told several important parables about lost sheep, the importance of forgiveness, and a story about workers in a vineyard that angered the Jewish leaders. He placed His hands on and blessed children, declaring, *"Let the children come to me, and do not prevent them; for the kingdom of heaven belongs to such as these."* [95] He recalls how these and other events angered the Pharisees, scribes, the High Priest, and the entire Sanhedrin.

Part Four

Yom Sheni, Monday, the second day, cleansing the temple in Jerusalem

Matthew sees and makes mental notes of many things he will someday write in his account. What Jesus did on this day finds a place in his written notes: *"Jesus entered the temple area and drove out all those engaged in selling and buying there. He overturned the tables of the money changers and the seats of those who were selling*

---

[95] Mt 19:14

doves. And he said to them, "It is written: 'My house shall be a house of prayer,' but you are making it a den of thieves." The blind and the lame approached him in the temple area, and he cured them. When the chief priests and the scribes saw the wondrous things he was doing, and the children crying out in the temple area, 'Hosanna to the Son of David,' they were indignant and said to him, 'Do you hear what they are saying?' Jesus said to them, 'Yes; and have you never read the text, 'Out of the mouths of infants and nurslings you have brought forth praise?' And leaving them, he went out of the city to Bethany, and there he spent the night."* [96] "Oh, Jesus," Matthew laments, "Did you have to do that?" He knows from experience the greed and covetousness of the money changers. They won't hesitate to throw hot, angry fuel on the fire of rage that awaits Jesus.

Part Five

Yom Shlishi, Tuesday, the third day, teaching the crowds and debating the Pharisees in the Temple area in Jerusalem, pronouncing seven woes

Matthew sees still more on this day to recall and write in his account, which he knows is stoking the flames of rage. Later that evening, he writes: *"Jesus said to them in reply, 'Amen, I say to you, if you have faith and do not waver, not only will you do what has been done to the fig tree, but even if you say to this mountain, 'Be lifted up and thrown into the sea,' it will be done. Whatever you ask*

---

[96] Mt 21:12-17

for in prayer with faith, you will receive." ⁹⁷ "Here we are climbing and counting mountaintop experiences, and Jesus is talking about having faith strong enough to command mountains to be thrown into the sea." Matthew is speaking to the disciples. He continues. "Brothers, John and I were discussing the woes Jesus pronounced on the scribes today. Did you notice how strongly Jesus denounced the scribes and Pharisees, telling everyone in the crowd to do as they say, not as they do? Don't be like them, seeking recognition as a rabbi or master. And then, brothers, you recall how he launched into the woes. There were seven. I know this because I counted them. I know. I am sorry, but I couldn't resist. Besides, John counted, too."

"Please continue, Matthew," Peter encourages him. "We understand."

Matthew takes a deep breath and says, "Six of the woes began thus, *Woe to you, scribes and Pharisees, you hypocrites.* ⁹⁸ The other began with, *Woe to you, blind guides,* which was just as condemnatory as the other six. That's not all. If you recall, Jesus also called them *blind fools, blind ones, blind Pharisees, and blind guides* a second time. Oh, and don't forget that He called them *serpents* and a *brood of vipers.*"

"Matthew," Peter interrupts, "none of this surprises me or anyone else here. Has Jesus ever spoken anything but truth?"

"I know," Matthew answers. "We just feel like he passed a point of no return with those seven woes."

---

⁹⁷ Mt 21:21-22
⁹⁸ See Mt 23:13-29 for this and the following 'woes.'

"You may be correct," Peter says, but have you let your worry distract you from an important detail that came out during the woes? Have you heard what He said about Abel and considered its implications?" Everyone needs to be reminded of the words, so Peter quotes them. *"Therefore, behold, I send to you prophets and wise men and scribes; some of them you will kill and crucify, some of them you will scourge in your synagogues and pursue from town to town, so that there may come upon you all the righteous blood shed upon earth, from the righteous blood of Abel to the blood of Zechariah, the son of Barachiah, whom you murdered between the sanctuary and the altar."* [99]

Matthew sits quietly while the rest look at him, expecting the idea to click. They had seen and discussed it earlier, but Matthew missed a detail that the others found important on this busy day.

Then, Peter says, "Do you recall our conversations about Abel during the Second Mountaintop experience? Who among us would not admit to having at least a twinge of doubt as to whether Abel and his parents, Adam and Eve, were real people, even after what Jesus taught concerning them? None of us dared to ask the Lord. All of us have heard the theories and speculations about the three of them being nothing more than symbolic figures, myths, and allegories added by the ancient scribes after being passed down orally for generations. Well, I submit that Jesus settled that question today. We should ask a question. Would Jesus feel and speak about a fictitious character in this way?"

---

[99] Mt 23:34-36

Having not yet picked up Peter's point, Matthew watches as everyone shakes their heads, No. "Exactly," Peter continues. "One doesn't have feelings like this for fictitious symbolic people. Besides, no one will suggest that Zechariah and Barachiah were not real people. Why single out Abel? Why doubt his historicity? The deaths of real prophets and people fueled Jesus's anger today, not some fictitious characters. Not only this but when we understand that Abel walked this earth, we must conclude that his parents, Adam and Eve, did too."

"Wow, Peter," says Matthew. "I have underestimated you."

"Well, Matthew, consider this. I've been a student of the best teacher of all time for nearly three years. I should hope to gain some spiritual wisdom. But please hear me out. I will continue to do some dumb and faithless things."

The rest of the disciples agreed, not about Peter assuredly doing dumb and faithless things, but about themselves assuredly doing dumb and faithless things.

"Yes," Nathaniel adds, "we should remember something else He said today. *Whoever exalts himself will be humbled; but whoever humbles himself will be exalted.*" [100]

"Anger wasn't the only feeling Jesus showed today," interjects James the Lesser. "He was profoundly sad. Recall his next words: *Jerusalem, Jerusalem, you who kill the prophets and stone those sent to you, how many times I yearned to gather your children together, as a hen gathers her young under her wings, but you were unwilling!*" [101]

---

[100] Mt 23:12
[101] Mt 23:37

Andrew adds, "Jesus was doing the same thing David did, lamenting for those who betray Him."

With this, all conversation ceases, and everyone finds a place to sleep. Tomorrow, they will make the final preparations to celebrate Passover. It would be their Last Supper together. That's what he said.

Part Six

Yom Revi'i, Wednesday, the fourth day, resting at the house of Martha, Mary, and Lazarus, preparing to celebrate the Passover

The Twelve return from Jerusalem as the sun is setting after another long, grueling day, the dark night closing in quickly. The cool air and cold water are a welcome respite from the heat and oppression that has steadily grown since they first entered Jerusalem just three days ago. Jesus approaches the Twelve. He knows they are reeling. He knows they need encouragement beyond what He can offer in words. He thinks ahead several days and realizes how dependent they will become on His presence, but not in the way they have experienced His presence over the past three years. He pauses in front of them and looks up. Sensing that he wants to teach them something, as He often does, through a non-verbal form of communication, they all look up.

The earth gracefully spins on its axis, and a celestial dance above Jerusalem unfolds with a mesmerizing rhythm. The sky, a vast canvas, begins to darken as Yom Revi'i draws to a close. The sun slowly dips below the horizon, casting a golden glow fading into twilight. Stars begin to twinkle, each one a distant beacon in the night. The constellations, ancient and eternal, shift in their positions, telling stories passed down through generations. Orion, the mighty hunter, stands tall in the sky, his belt of three stars a familiar sight. To the west lies Taurus, the bull charging forward, its bright red eye, Aldebaran, gleaming fiercely. As the night deepens, the constellations continue their silent march across the heavens. The Pleiades, a cluster of seven sisters, shimmer delicately, their light a reminder of the myths and legends that have shaped human understanding of the cosmos. The Milky Circle, a river of stars, flows across the sky, a celestial pathway connecting the past with the present. The hypnotic reverie has its desired effect, a firm and deep realization that the Master is in control. Does not He, who controls wind and waves, not also control the celestial elements? Did He not create this also? Yes, the disciples feel a deep and abiding comfort. Most of them will sleep well tonight, the exception being Matthew.

There is much to catalog. The days following Jesus' first entry into Jerusalem have been very busy and full of spiritually significant events. Matthew thanks John for any measure of sanity he retains. There had been the 'triumphal' Jerusalem entry, the cleansing of the temple, the curing of the blind and lame, the cursing of a fig tree, seeing it withered the next day, and "the lesson" to be learned from the fig tree, that it symbolized Israel's spiritual barrenness. There had been many parables, the one about two sons in the vineyard, one who promised but did not work and the other who did work, the parable about the landowner with a vineyard and his tenants who seized his servants and even his son, whom they killed to acquire his inheritance, the parable of the wedding feast and how the guest without a wedding garment was *"cast into the darkness outside, where there will be wailing and grinding of teeth."* [102]

Matthew has watched with ominous dread as things went from bad to worse with the religious leaders. Does Jesus not see that He is inciting the very men who could easily incite the crowd to turn on Him? Does He not see the scribe's indignation when they saw the wondrous things and heard the *"children cry out in the temple area, 'Hosanna to the Son of David?'"* [103] Why did he say to them, *"Yes; and have you never read the text, 'Out of the mouths of infants and nurslings you have brought forth praise?'"* [104] And then, there had been the lengthy discourse on the Mount of Olives concerning the end times, his second coming, and the seven woes.

So, Matthew spent much of the night and the next day obsessing over details. John spent much of the day trying to calm him down. Peter spent much of the day preparing for what Matthew could not tell. Judas spent the day counting the money. The other disciples spent the day wandering around, almost aimless, deep in thought one moment, paralyzed with fear the next.

Matthew does his best to live in the moment but regresses when he recalls another series of scenes related to the number seven. Towards evening, he pulls John aside to discuss it. "I want to discuss another series of scenes that caught my attention, especially because of their association with the number seven. They started in Judea, across the Jordan, after we had left Galilee

---

[102] Mt 22:13
[103] Mt 21:15b-
[104] Mt 21:16

and after Peter's seven-based forgiveness question. After this, the Sadducees, who do not believe in the resurrection, tried to trick Jesus with a question about divorce and remarriage. The question they contrived concerned seven brothers and one woman who married them all because after one died, she would marry the next until all seven had died. He astonished them and the crowd with His answer. *You are misled because you do not know the scriptures or the power of God. At the resurrection they neither marry nor are given in marriage but are like the angels in heaven. And concerning the resurrection of the dead, have you not read what was said to you by God, 'I am the God of Abraham, the God of Isaac, and the God of Jacob'? He is not the God of the dead but of the living."* [105]

Matthew continues. "Did you hear the exchange after Jesus silenced the Pharisees while they were still gathered? Let me quote it. *'What is your opinion about the Messiah? Whose son is he?'* They replied, *'David's.' He said to them, 'How, then, does David, inspired by the Spirit, call him 'lord,' saying: 'The Lord said to my lord, 'Sit at my right hand until I place your enemies under your feet'? If David calls him 'lord,' how can he be his son?* [106] Do you see what Jesus has done, John? He has led them right to the Archetype of the Seventh Blessing, showing them that David, who they claim as the greatest king of Israel, is the same man who calls Him, 'my Lord.' It is a claim that riles them to the point of no return. There can be no reconciliation between the religious leaders and Jesus."

John picks up the train of thought. "Yes, Matthew, it was after this confrontation that Jesus pronounced those seven woes.

---

[105] Mt 22:29-32
[106] Mt 22:42-46

I didn't miss the seven counts of which you speak. I, too, sense that he has pushed them too far. Each woe was a provocative and public condemnation against the religious leaders. Everyone saw it. Everyone heard it and saw their reactions and discerned their motives, their plotting for revenge, their plans to have him killed."

Matthew's voice rises as he cries, "What are we to do?"

Jesus was off somewhere by Himself, so He didn't hear it. However, the other disciples were much closer, and they heard Matthew. They walk over to join the two contemplatives. They see Matthew with tears streaming down his face and John's hand on his shoulder, the younger consoling the elder. No one says anything for ten minutes.

Finally, Peter speaks up and asks, "Matthew, is there something you want to share with us?"

Matthew motions for everyone to sit down. It is late, but no one moves while he rehashes everything he and John have just discussed.

Jesus returns just as Matthew finishes one of his lengthier monologues. He pauses and looks up again. The disciples look up, too, in time to see the first light of dawn break over Jerusalem, casting a soft, rosy hue across the landscape. Were they awake all night?

And then, as Yom Revi'i gives way to Yom Chamishi, the sky begins to lighten once more. The constellations slowly fade, their stories temporarily hidden by the approaching dawn. The earth continues its steady rotation, bringing the promise of a new day. The celestial elements, having played their part in the grand tapestry of time, retreat until the next night, when they will once again grace the sky with their timeless beauty. The group is walking to Jerusalem, to the Upper Room, where they will gather to observe and participate in Passover, a nearly 1500-year-old tradition celebrating God's deliverance of the Israelites from Egyptian bondage. They will gather for what Jesus has been calling 'the Last Supper.' The air is filled with anticipation and reverence, but so, too, fear as the occasion's significance descends upon them.

CHAPTER 8

CONTEMPLATING THE EIGHTH

And when they came to a place called Golgotha (which means Place of the Skull), they gave Jesus wine to drink mixed with gall. But when he had tasted it, he refused to drink. After they had crucified him, they divided his garments by casting lots; then they sat down and kept watch over him there. And they placed over his head the written charge against him: This is Jesus, the King of the Jews. Two revolutionaries were crucified with him, one on his right and the other on his left. [107]

---

[107] Mt 27:33-38

Part Seven

Spring, AD 30: 14th day of Nisan, late evening, Yom Chamishi, Thursday, the fifth day, the first day of the Feast of Unleavened Bread, the Upper Room in Jerusalem, celebrating the Passover, the Last Supper

When it was evening, he reclined at table with the Twelve. And while they were eating, he said, 'Amen, I say to you, one of you will betray me.' Deeply distressed at this, they began to say to him one after another, 'Surely it is not I, Lord?' He said in reply, 'He who has dipped his hand into the dish with me is the one who will betray me. The Son of Man indeed goes, as it is written of him, but woe to that man by whom the Son of Man is betrayed. It would be better for that man if he had never been born.' Then Judas, his betrayer, said in reply, 'Surely it is not I, Rabbi?' He answered, 'You have said so.' While they were eating, Jesus took bread, said the blessing, broke it, and giving it to his disciples said, 'Take and eat; this is my body.' Then he took a cup, gave thanks, and gave it to them, saying, 'Drink from it, all of you, for this is my blood of the covenant, which will be shed on behalf of many for the forgiveness of sins. I tell you, from now on I shall not drink this fruit of the vine until the day when I drink it with you new in the Kingdom of my Father.' Then, after singing a hymn, they went out to the Mount of Olives. [108]

---

[108] Mt 26:20-30

Part Eight

AD 30: midnight, Yom Shishi, the sixth day, in the Garden of Gethsemane on the Mount of Olives

The eleven and Jesus arrive at the Mount of Olives. The air is chilly. The sky is dark and starless. Heavy, ominous clouds shroud the full moon, muffling its proud glow and causing it to cast long, eerie, lifeless shadows below. Matthew and John, the last to arrive, find a place to sit. They are tired. They are all tired. Matthew is fearful and confused. He thinks of the conversation John and he had on the way from the upper room to here. He doesn't want to, but he feels that he has to. So much has gone wrong tonight. First, Jesus had said that one of them would betray Him. Matthew, perhaps because he never stopped watching the money bags, had an idea who that might be before Judas asked Jesus if it was him, and Jesus replied, *You have said so.* [109] After Judas left, Jesus said something about their faith in Him being shaken and quoted Zechariah. Is it all falling apart? Matthew frets. He seriously wonders if even Jesus is losing it. "John," he says, "you know as well as I do that the Lord forgot the fourth cup."

"I don't think He forgot," says John." It seemed like He intentionally delayed it when He said, *I tell you, from now on I shall not drink this fruit of the vine until the day when I drink it with you new in the kingdom of my Father.*" [110]

---

[109] Mt 26:25b
[110] Mt 26:29

"Yes," says Matthew, "and right after that, we came here to the Mount of Olives." "It's so odd," says John, "but I feel certain He knew what He was doing. Recall that we did sing the Hallel Psalms."

The two sit there quietly. After a few minutes, Jesus calls Peter, James, and John to follow Him a short way to the Garden of Gethsemane. At that moment, Matthew hears a rumble of thunder and feels an ominous chilly gust. He watches the four of them walk away. He is a mess.

Cringing with anxiety, Matthew, as was his habit at times like this, lapses into perseverating over problems related to numbers and other questions, replaying past conversations in his mind, conversations he has replayed far too many times already. On some nights like this one, he carries on a full conversation, speaking for the other imaginary figure or figures.

"John, don't you see how the arrangement of numbers and words must be correct, or the meaning can change substantially? Seveny-seven times means one thing. Seventy times seven means another. Moving the word "times" from the end to the middle of that three-word phrase makes a difference."

Imagining, well in point of fact, recalling John's response, he replays his next statement. "Here is another number problem posed by scripture. 1 Chronicles lists and numbers Jesse's sons explicitly calling Eliab his firstborn, Abinadab the second, Shimea the third, Nethanel the fourth, Raddai the fifth, Ozem the sixth, and David the seventh. [111] However, 1 Samuel tells how Jesse

---

[111] 1 Chr 2:13-15

made seven of his sons pass before Samuel, and then David, the youngest, was called in from tending the sheep, making him the eighth son. [112] Which one is it?"

He interrupts his monologue to upbraid himself. "Oh, come on, Matthew- really, tonight, of all nights, you want to ruminate over that question again."

He ignores the reprimand and continues rehashing the past conversation. "It's an important question, John, even now. It matters for many reasons, not the least of which is the archetypal numbering we have discussed over the past few years. In my opinion, David must be the seventh son, and the book of Samuel must be wrong."

"Matthew," John had responded, "Did you say God's word is wrong- that's hard to believe. Have you considered that the ambiguity may be intentional? We agree that God inspired the men of old to write them, and we know He does not make mistakes. Think with me, for a moment, about the seventh and eighth blessings. The seventh, if it represents completion and perfection as it does elsewhere in scripture, could be understood as the last blessing. I see your question, Matthew, but hold on. If the seventh is last, why can't the eighth be seen as a summation of the prior seven? It doesn't add anything new per se but rather summarizes the state of the person who has journeyed through the seven and, in the process, becomes a person who manifests the eighth. Look at the reward of the eighth blessing; *Theirs is the kingdom of heaven.* [113] You and I have discussed this. It is the same

---

[112] 1 Sm 16:10-11
[113] Mt 5:10b

reward as the first blessing. So, he, who starts with the first and progresses through the next six to complete the seventh, arrives again at the eighth."

John had stopped, Matthew had thought, and then he had spoken. "Yes," he thought, still rehashing the conversation, "I did take time to think before responding to you, John. You know, John, I recall that Jesus had stressed that we should not get overly fixated on rigidly assigning various archetypes to one blessing."

"You've got it, Matthew," the younger had said as he playfully patted the elder on the back. "I am proud of you for freeing yourself from another fixation. Moreover, Jesus has repeatedly stressed how everyone, archetypes, disciples, and anyone who wants to follow Him must progress from one blessing to the next as part of their journey to holiness."

"Yes, I see all of that," Matthew had interrupted. "Still, we should expect to find another man who is the archetype of the eighth blessing, and the ninth, for that matter. Who is it?"

It takes a lot of mental energy to replay such scenes, and Matthew is tired. Peering through the foggy air towards the Garden, he spots Jesus motioning for the three to wait as He moves further into the Garden by Himself. The fog thickens, and a mist hides the four completely from view. Matthew pulls his mantel over his head, curls up next to a rock, and starts praying, "Lord have mercy. Lord have mercy, Lord have mercy." After repeating this perhaps fifteen times, he drifts into a deep sleep, and shortly after, he begins to dream.

In his dream, Matthew and the other disciples are watching a play in a garden at the bottom of a large amphitheater. The performance starts in utter darkness, followed by a sudden bright light and a thundering bang, so loud in the dream that it nearly wakes Matthew. After a heavy mist clears, a man and a woman step forward and listen while the Son of Man says, *"Blessed are the poor in spirit, for theirs is the kingdom of heaven,"* [114] to which they respond gleefully, *"Our Father in heaven."* [115] Immediately, the stage becomes pitch black, and there is silence, followed by another flash of light- the next act follows.

Two brothers step forward. The larger clubs the other over the head with a rock and leaves him lying in a pool of blood, dead. After the murderer leaves, the Son of Man comes forward and touches the victim, resurrects the man, and says, *"Blessed are they who mourn, for they will be comforted,"* [116] to which the man joyfully exclaims, *"Hallowed be thy name."* [117] Again, silence and darkness, followed by a flash of light and a rainbow filling the sky- the third act follows.

A third man stands while his wife, three sons, and their wives wait in the background. The Son of Man appears and says, *"Blessed are the meek, for they shall inherit the earth."* [118] The third man and his family step forward and incredulously answer, *"Thy kingdom come, thy will be done on earth as it is in heaven."* [119] At that moment, the Son of Man raises his hand and lifts a gigantic veil to reveal that this third man and his family are standing on a giant mountain, a mountain so high that it joins earth and heaven.

---

[114] Mt 5:3
[115] Mt 6:9
[116] Mt 5:4
[117] Mt 6:9b
[118] Mt 5:5
[119] Mt 6:10

Matthew and the others in his dream gasp with delight. They also realize that the prior two scenes and every scene will take place on a mountain. Silence, darkness, light- the fourth act follows.

A fourth man with his firstborn son of the promise behind him steps forward. The Son of Man says, *"Blessed are they who hunger and thirst for righteousness, for they shall be satisfied."* [120] The fourth man looks to his right and sees a very old but distinguished king and priest holding bread and wine. The fourth man and his son look to their left and see a lamb stuck in a thicket. The fourth man with his son of the covenant rejoice exceedingly, *"Give us this day our daily bread."* [121] Silence, darkness, light- the fifth act follows.

A grave in Shechem opens, and a skeleton jumps out. A flash of heavenly rainbow light fills it, and a young man wearing a beautiful coat of many colors steps forward. Behind him, there are seventy people, an elderly man nearing death with eleven sons, their wives and concubines, and their animals. The Son of Man says, *"Blessed are the merciful, for they shall receive mercy."* [122] The man wearing the many-colored coat looks back at the seventy behind him and motions for them to join him. Together, they confidently pray, *"Forgive us our trespasses, as we forgive those who trespass against us."* [123] Silence, darkness, light- the sixth act follows.

A white-bearded man holds high a bronze serpent so that anyone who looks at it may be saved from snake bites in the desert

---

[120] Mt 5:6
[121] Mt 6:11
[122] Mt 5:7
[123] Mt 6:12 (quoting Matthew but using 'trespasses' as the prayer is said in Mass)

wilderness. Now, he is carrying the Staff of God and standing on a tall mountain, at the base of which stands over 600,000 men with their wives and children. His face is shining. The Son of Man approaches them and says, *"Blessed are the clean of heart, for they shall see God."* [124] The man at the top of the mountain and the crowd at the bottom move across a vast sea. When they reach the other side, they sing thunderously a new song to the LORD, *"Lead us not into temptation."* [125] Silence, darkness, light- the seventh act follows.

A mighty warrior king wearing a linen ephod, followed by seventy others carrying the Ark of the Lord, and 500,000 people from the Twelve Tribes of Israel march forward victoriously into the Holy City, the city now named the City of David, the place where God will dwell with men to be their God and they to be His people. The Son of Man approaches them and says, *"Blessed are the peacemakers, for they will be called children of God."* [126] At that moment, the 500,000 dance mightily before the Son of Man, singing, *"And deliver us from evil"* [127] Silence, darkness, but light did not follow- the eighth act follows.

Matthew shifts uncomfortably in his sleep and pulls his mantel over his exposed shoulder. His eyes are closed, but Matthew can't decide whether he is asleep and dreaming or awake and praying. With his eyes closed, he watches and understands through the Spirit that time hasn't stopped. It has merged, has reached back

---

[124] Mt 5:8
[125] Mt 6:13a (quoting Matthew as the phrase is used in Mass)
[126] Mt 5:9
[127] Mt 6:13 (quoting Matthew as the phrase is used in Mass)

2,500 years, and forward 1,500 years. It may have seemed like four thousand years compressed into a moment, but only four seconds elapsed, for that's how fast time moves in dreams. Matthew looks around and sees that everyone has left the amphitheater. He watches and understands he is left in the amphitheater of his mind to watch the eighth scene alone.

The mood feels decidedly somber, the heavy, persistent darkness oppressive. Light appears, not bright but suppressed, creeping stealthily over the scene before Matthew. Matthew cringes as he looks at the sky and sees ominous clouds shrouding the full moon, muffling its proud glow and causing it to cast long, eerie, lifeless shadows over the amphitheater below. The air is chilly. The night is starless. He watches the amphitheater intently, although, truthfully, he thought he might rather run. A shrouded figure steps onto the stage. More correctly, the figure appears to glide or float across the stage, a phenomenon Matthew attributes to its feet being covered by the long draping linen ephod, so one could not see its steps. Still, he cowers before the phantomlike figure, barely managing to raise his eyes to look at it. He recognizes some of its clothing, the linen tunic, just visible under the ephod, a colorful camel's hide sash around its' waist. Why did the waist appear so prominent? He recognizes the linen undergarments running from its' waist to its' thighs. There, he saw it again. What was the hump projecting from its' front? Was it a woman, and was she pregnant? It was an odd mixture, to say the least, a pregnant woman portrayed as a death-filled phantom. But wait; this priest had to be a man. Then he hears a voice. It says, 'The woman's time, her part in this unfolding drama, is yet to come.' Matthew watches tremulously as the Son of Man approaches the phantom and slowly places

His hand on the top of the turban covering the phantom's head. Wait, was the hand pierced, and was it bleeding? The Son of Man quickly jerks the shroud up and off, exposing the mysterious man underneath. A boom fills the air, as did exceedingly bright light. It is painfully bright. Matthew's eyes burn, and he wants to close them but can't. He had no choice but to look at the eighth priestly figure. Matthew recoils in abject horror. He would have fainted, but he couldn't do that because he was flat on the ground asleep. Still, he dreamt that he fell to the ground even as he lay on it beneath his shroud. The figure in front of him was headless. More precisely, it held its head on a platter and offered it to the Son of Man, who said, *"Blessed are they who are persecuted for the sake of righteousness, for theirs is the kingdom of heaven."* [128] And then the eighth man, the priest, prayed. Matthew could not tell where the words came from, whether from the mouth on the head on the platter or from the Son of Man. Perhaps it came from both. They, He, said, *"Deliver us, Lord, we pray, from every evil, graciously grant peace in our days, that, by the help of your mercy, we may be always free from sin and safe from all distress, as we await the blessed hope and the coming of our Savior, Jesus Christ."* [129] The bright light intensified.

In his dream/awake state, Matthew pulls his shroud over his head, trying to hide from the bright light in the amphitheater of his mind. It is a futile undertaking. Prompted again by the Spirit, Matthew immediately understands on some level that he has to

---

[128] Mt 10:10

[129] Quoting from Mass how the Priest prays the embolism in 'Persona Christi' after the congregants finish the first seven parts of the Lord's Prayer

learn that prayer to suffer for the sake of righteousness. He racks his brain desperately. Where had he heard those words, and who was the headless priest? The brightness of the light and the heat it emitted bore down on him, bore into his eyes. Still, he could not close them or look away. Wait, he had heard those words earlier that evening during the Passover meal. He was sure of it. The brightness and heat intensified. Had Jesus taught them at some earlier time? No, he clearly recalled that He had not said them during the Sermon on the Mount.

The brightness and heat intensified. When Matthew thinks he can bear it no more, the burning brightness searing his body and soul, Matthew suddenly realizes that he is awake. He is drenched in sweat and suddenly chilled, despite or because of his shroud, shaking, quaking with an odd mix of fear and wonder. Prompted by the Spirit a third time, he marvels to himself and says. "John the Baptist was the headless man and is the Archetype of the Eighth Blessing!" Matthew is stunned by this sudden realization. Why didn't I see this before?" He recalls what Jesus had said about John the Baptist over two years ago. *"Behold, I am sending my messenger ahead of you; he will prepare your way before you. Amen, I say to you, among those born of women there has been none greater than John the Baptist; yet the least in the kingdom of heaven is greater than he. From the days of John the Baptist until now, the kingdom of heaven suffers violence, and the violent are taking it by force."* [130]

He saw that violence in his dream and again that night when they arrested Jesus. Then, Matthew thought of the many ways

---

[130] Mt 11:10-12

Jesus had followed John. John preceded Him in birth by six months. [131] John preceded Him in proclaiming how the kingdom of heaven will be ushered in when he said, *"Repent, for the kingdom of heaven is at hand."* [132] Would Jesus follow John, who had died a violent death for the sake of righteousness?

Then, he remembers Jesus' next words concerning Elijah and John. *"All the prophets and the law prophesied up to the time of John. And if you are willing to accept it, he is Elijah, the one who is to come. Whoever has ears ought to hear."* [133] The Transfiguration scene on the sixth mountain flashes forward and floods his mind with questions. He cries in his dream. These urgent questions must be answered urgently, but he senses that he is awakening from the dream. He closes his eyes tightly, concentrates intently, and catalogs the questions. If John is the greatest among those born of women and yet less than the least in the kingdom of heaven, what happened to him at death?

Then he asks, did Elijah or John the Baptist appear on the Mountain of Transfiguration? Was it both? Many considered Elijah to be the greatest of the prophets. He did not die. He was taken up to heaven in a whirlwind by a fiery chariot and fiery horses. [134] John the Baptist died violently but quickly. Was he in heaven in the same instant? If John is Elijah, should Jesus be considered a type of Elisha who was to come? Matthew thought about the question, but he did not, and he could not engage with

---

[131] Lk 1:35-36
[132] Mt 3:2 and Mt 4:17
[133] Mt 11:13-15
[134] 2 Kgs 2:11

it or think about it for even a moment. Instead, he pondered the idea conveyed in his dream that the prayer Jesus taught them in the Sermon is supposed to be a word-for-word appeal to have the blessings manifest in one's life, even the eighth blessing. And John the Baptist is the Archetype of the Eighth Blessing. Am I, are we, his disciples, destined to die violent deaths? He shudders violently as this question settles on him.

Matthew looks up and sees Jesus facing Judas, the betrayer, accompanied by a large crowd with swords and clubs, who had come from the chief priests and the elders of the people to arrest Jesus. Had he slept for hours or minutes? Matthew couldn't tell. He was, indeed, alone. The other disciples had fled. Too ashamed to look into Jesus' eyes, for he felt he had done enough of that already, Matthew jumps up and runs. He would learn later from John, the younger Son of Thunder, and Mary, Jesus' mother, how Jesus was arrested, tried, mocked, spit upon, beaten, crowned with thorns, stripped naked, and made to carry a cross. Matthew would learn later from them how Jesus' eighth mountaintop experience came to an end in the third hour, that Jesus was nailed to a cross on Golgotha, the place of the skull, outside the city walls of first-century Jerusalem, on Mount Moriah where Abraham was instructed to sacrifice his son Isaac, formerly where Melchizedek, King of Salem, offered bread and wine to Abraham. He would learn from them later that darkness covered the earth in the sixth hour. He would learn later from them the nine last words Jesus spoke and the nine times he exhaled while hanging for six hours on the cross from the third hour until the ninth hour. It is another nine-related observation, but investigating its meaning will have to wait.

CHAPTER 9

CONTEMPLATING THE NINTH

The eleven disciples went to Galilee, to the mountain to which Jesus had ordered them. [135]

Early morning, circa AD 30: Yom Chamishi, forty days after the resurrection of Jesus Christ from the dead, in Bethany on the Mount of Olivet

It is a glorious, hope-filled spring morning with a brilliant blue sky. The sun is rising to bathe the world in a warm, golden glow. The air is filled with the sweet scent of blooming Nicotiana and Lily of the Valley. The joyful chirping of new hatchlings and the playful scurrying of small animals bring the scene to life. These

---

[135] Mt 28:16

splendors of nature go unnoticed by Matthew today. Usually the one to bring up the rear, he is now at the forefront, his sandals kicking up dust as he races ahead of the other disciples. He is running uphill. His eyes are fixed on the summit of the ninth mountain, where he knows Jesus awaits. His heart pounds with a singular focus: to reach Jesus. He is driven by an eagerness that propels him forward with every step. The other disciples walk energetically, their cheerful voices adding to the orchestra of life, but they soon give up trying to run with Matthew.

Matthew sees Jesus. "Lord," he whispers while falling to his knees. The others catch up, and they do the same to a man. There is much to talk about and many questions to answer, especially numerological questions, and there is much to do. However, silence is the best word for this moment; worship is the only proper act. Still, they doubt, so Jesus approaches and says, *"All power in heaven and on earth has been given to me. Go, therefore, and make disciples of all nations, baptizing them in the name of the Father, and of the Son, and of the holy Spirit, teaching them to observe all that I have commanded you. And behold, I am with you always, until the end of the age."* [136]

Jesus words reach Matthew's ears, settle in his mind, and pierce his soul. He wonders but doesn't say, should I start counting again? Keeping silent still, he thinks, we are on the ninth mountain, Lord, but when I hear you say 'Baptize,' I think of beginnings. I think of firsts and starts and…, What is it, Lord? Then, it comes to him, and he shouts out, "rebirths."

---

[136] Mt 28:18-20

His own spoken words shake him out of his reverie, and he looks up. With the others, he watches Jesus rise. As he ascends out of sight, a cloud takes him from their sight. They suddenly see two men dressed in white garments next to them. They say, *"'Men of Galilee, why are you standing there looking at the sky? This Jesus who has been taken up from you into heaven will return in the same way as you have seen him going into heaven.' Then they returned to Jerusalem from the Mount called Olivet, which is near Jerusalem, a sabbath day's journey away."* [137]

Matthew counted as he and the others descended from the ninth mountain. He counted and contemplated for the duration of the Sabbath day's journey that a trek from the Mount called Olivet to the Upper Room in Jerusalem normally takes, mind you, when one is walking, not sprinting as the first trek that day had occurred.

He and John speak. "When I write a gospel someday," Matthew says, "I shall begin with Jesus beginnings, describing his genealogy, including, of course, his mother and father and the various details of the journey they took to Egypt and back, and other things."

John responds, "That sounds interesting. What will you call the first mountain?"

Matthew thinks a moment and responds. "I will call it Bethlehem, but I won't use the word mountain."

"Why not," John asks.

Matthew answers, "Because, just as I won't use the word mountain to describe the eighth mountain of Jesus life, the one

---

[137] Acts 1:11

on which he was crucified, the one where he died, so too, I won't use the word mountain in describing the first."

John ponders this and says, "I like it, Matthew. Still, to give your readers a hint when they one day look to understand this nine-part construct of your gospel, you may want to emphasize the word Bethlehem."

"Great idea," Matthew responds. "I will write Bethlehem more than once, perhaps even four times in a short space of the gospel." [138]

John asks another question. "How shall you end it, Matthew?"

Matthew replies. "I'm not sure about the very end, except to say that I will describe what we did here today and, of course, the other eight mountaintop experiences of Jesus life."

John responds, "I figured you would do that, Matthew, but my question was directed at the beginning of your gospel. Let me rephrase it. How will you finish the first part of your gospel, the part in which you describe Jesus beginning?"

Matthew smiles and says, "You are a clever young man. I see what you are getting at. I will finish my story of Jesus first mountaintop experience with his Baptism by John the Baptist. Baptism is where the journey for the new believers starts. You heard Him say it today, *Baptizing them in the name of the Father, the Son, and the Holy Spirit*. Do you see, John, why this makes perfect sense? The first Blessing, *Blessed are the poor in spirit, for theirs is the kingdom of heaven*, ends the same way as the eighth, *Blessed are they who are persecuted for the sake of righteousness, for theirs is the kingdom of heaven*."

---

[138] See Mt 2:1-6

John smiles. "I like that too, Matthew. It makes me wonder. When believers are baptized into our Lord's life, meaning they are 'born from above,' are they also in some way baptized into His death?"

Matthew thought about this question, especially in the context of the end of his dream. John the Baptist witnessed to Jesus. John was martyred. Jesus calls us to witness. He shudders.

John, the brother of James, brings him back to the present, asking his favorite question. "Will you keep counting?"

Matthew smiles and responds, "I am a retired tax collector. How can I ever stop counting? Still, I think Jesus has called me today to start counting again with the number one."

John ponders this and then says, "Matthew, he said he would be with us until the end of the age. What do you think He means by that?"

Matthew thinks for a minute and responds, "Do you remember the story His mother told us about John the Baptist and his words to the Pharisees?"

"I think I see where you are headed," John says. Both cringe as the word headed comes out, driving them to consider he who was beheaded.

John recovers and says, "Let me quote the words, *I am baptizing you with water, for repentance, but the one who is coming after me is mightier than I. I am not worthy to carry his sandals. He will baptize you with the holy Spirit and fire.*" [139]

---

[139] Mt 3:11

John's words reach Matthew's ears, settle in his mind, and pierce his soul. John's spoken words reach his own ears, settle in his own mind, and pierce his own soul.

Matthew doesn't know why, but the Baptist's words bring great comfort. John has the same experience.

A sense of awe fills their souls. The next moment, they find themselves on the ground, on their knees, looking up. They are at the base of the Mount called Olivet, looking up and quietly worshipping God in their interior space. What else is there to do? Worship is the only proper act for this moment. The two contemplatives don't say another word for the rest of the journey back to the Upper Room, but they do contemplate, and they do count.

CHAPTER 10

THE FIRST REVELATION OF THE NINTH ARCHETYPE OF THE NINTH BLESSING – THE TENTH MOUNTAINTOP EXPERIENCE

They did him homage and then returned to Jerusalem with great joy, and they were continually in the temple praising God. [140]

Part One

Spring, AD 30: forty-nine days after Jesus' resurrection, nine days after His ascension, early morning, Yom Shabbat, the seventh day, in the Upper Room in Jerusalem,

---

[140] Lk 24: 52-53

devoting themselves with one accord to prayer, together with some women, and Mary the mother of Jesus and his brothers, waiting to receive power from the Holy Spirit.

After his ascension, the disciples stayed in the Upper Room on the mountain on which Jerusalem is located. It is early morning. The earth rotates on its axis, bringing those assembled in the Upper Room face to face with the rising sun. The disciples, the mother of Jesus, and others have been there for nine days since Jesus' ascension. They have prayed much. They have discussed many things. They have learned from Cleopas and another disciple about the dinner after a long hike to Emmaus on the same day of His resurrection, about how Jesus had interpreted all the scriptures that referred to him from Moses and all the prophets, and then how they failed to recognize him until he was with them *"at the table, took bread, said the blessing, broke it, and gave it to them."* [141] Who could forget Thomas touching his wounds and saying, *"My Lord and my God?"* [142] Peter was originally distressed but then understood why Jesus asked him three times, *"Peter, do you love me,"* and told him *"to feed and tend to His sheep."* [143]

They are waiting and trying to understand His words, *"And behold, I am with you always, until the end of the age."* [144] John looks forward to living in Ephesus with Mary, the mother of Jesus. He is certain that conversations with her would allow him to find answers

---

[141] Lk 24:13-35
[142] Jn 20:28
[143] Jn 21:15-17
[144] Mt 28:20b

to many of his questions while, at the same time, providing him with a distinctly unique picture of the relationship between God and humanity, and not just any humanity, but that of the Son of God and his mother. Each Apostle has special memories that will help them fulfill the mission he has commissioned. And yet, all would need more than memories. They know it. How would they possibly do all these things, go to the ends of the earth, proclaim his message, and dispense the special blessings he has bestowed on them? How will they do all of this without him?

And then there is Matthew. Not surprisingly, he has numerous numerological questions. He fully agreed with replacing Judas to keep the Apostles at twelve. He pondered the 'fourth cup' question and tried to relate the Passover to the New Covenant meal Jesus had instituted. He contemplated the idea of worshipping on the eighth day when a week has only seven days. Was it another example of the eighth meeting the first? He also contemplated the eighth part of the prayer Jesus had taught them and wondered when they would learn the ninth part. He ponders all of these questions and others. Still, none occupies his time and imagination as much as the question of the identity of the Archetype of the Ninth Blessing.

They had been fasting for nine days since their last meal with Jesus, the risen Son, who had prepared a breakfast of fish and bread for them while they were fishing the Sea of Galilee.

"Moses fasted for forty days, not once but twice," Peter reminds the group.

"Speaking of fasting," Matthew says, "I recall very well when the Lord called me." James, the other son of thunder, speaks. "Of course, you would remember that brother, for it was on that blessed day that Jesus called you to join us."

Matthew smiles and reminisces. "The Pharisees couldn't understand why Jesus, who called himself Messiah, would eat with tax collectors and sinners like me."

Andrew speaks next. "Not long after that, the disciples of John the Baptist approached him and asked, *Why do we and the Pharisees fast much, but your disciples do not fast.*" [145]

John beams with joy as a new thought suddenly descends on him. "Brothers, how glorious his words that followed. *Can the wedding guests mourn as long as the bridegroom is with them? The days will come when the bridegroom is taken away from them, and then they will fast.*" [146]

The others understand how the fasting part of the Baptist's words fit into the conversation. Still, they wonder why John is so excited about the wedding and bridegroom talk.

Peter speaks. "Yes, we are fasting, as we should, as He instructed us to. I am convinced He will answer our prayers for the Spirit to descend on us and that Jesus will join us at that blessed time."

John responds. "Yes, He will join us in some mysterious way when the Spirit comes upon us with power."

"And, let me guess, John," Peter answers. "You think that we, his disciples, are in some way His bride?"

"That's right," John says. Moreover, we are also His body in some mysterious way." Immediately after John says this, the room fills with animated chatter, discussions, arguments, and debates.

After a bit, Peter stands up and says, "Brothers, what John has said does agree with what our Lord said when we celebrated

---

[145] Mt 9:14
[146] Mt 9:15

Passover with Him a year ago: *I am the living bread that came down from heaven; whoever eats this bread will live forever; and the bread that I will give is my flesh for the life of the world.* [147] Let's keep praying. If John is correct, God will make it clear to us."

Matthew speaks next. "Brothers, perhaps we should approach the question logically."

"Of course," the others say at once and at the same time, "We should count and contemplate."

"Matthew chuckles and says, "Oh my, have I trained you well. We should contemplate, but we don't need to count again."

The entire group is flabbergasted, laughing heartily at the counter's admission.

Regaining his poise, Peter says, "You've taught us well? Did you just say we don't need to count again? We never expected to hear those words out of your mouth. No brother, we have trained you well."

Matthew joins the laughter and then picks up the train of thought. "What I mean is that Jesus led us to the ninth mountain already. What lies before us now is the question…" Before Matthew can finish his sentence, the others say, "Who is the Archetype of the Ninth Blessing."

"Music to my ears," says Matthew.

As the last laugh echoes off the walls of the Upper Room, the room falls silent. After ten or so minutes, John looks at the mother of Jesus and smiles. "Mother," he says with a wink, shall we tell them about Jesus's last words on the cross."

---

[147] Jn 6:51

"Yes, Son, let's do that," she responds with another wink. Everyone is caught off guard. They had not previously heard them refer to each other as 'son' and 'mother.'

"All right," Phillip says, "Somebody has some explaining to do." The others nod their heads in agreement. What are these two talking about? When did they start calling each other mother and son?

John starts, for Mary prefers to speak little and pray much., which she does now. "Let me start by saying Jesus spoke nine times while he hung on that cross. Well, to be clear, He spoke words we could understand eight times. The ninth vocal utterance to leave His mouth was a loud cry that did not contain words. I see your eyes lighting up, Matthew. We will discuss these nine utterances on another day. Today, we must focus on just two because they will help answer your question. Listen to me carefully as I describe the scene, and believe me, because I was there. I saw it with my own two eyes and heard it with my own two ears. Listen, all of you, and believe. If you have any questions, Thomas, ask His mother. She was there, too, and something tells me none of us should doubt her. Now, let me tell you what happened.

Standing by the cross of Jesus were his mother and his mother's sister, Mary the wife of Clopas, and Mary of Magdala. When Jesus saw his mother and the disciple there whom he loved, he said to his mother, 'Woman, behold, your son.' Then he said to the disciple, 'Behold, your mother.'" [148]

---

[148] Jn 19: 25-27a

James, the son of Alphaeus, asks, "To be clear, you are not her son biologically? You aren't revealing some hidden family scandal that may have explained why Jesus loved you so much?"

Matthew thinks, "If one of our own still questions her integrity, what will the Pharisees think? I must include those four women in the genealogy."

John answers, "Correct, James. I am her son in a far greater way, spiritually."

"Hold on a minute," says Nathaneal, "let's not talk about who is greatest. If my memory serves me right, Jesus corrected your biological mother, you, and your brother James here for wanting to be the closest to our Lord. [149] So now, you are taking a second shot at it and claiming to be the Mother of Our Lord's son in a far greater way than the rest of us."

"Look, brothers," John says earnestly, "He asked me to live with her so I can take care of her. She's a widow who lost her only son. That's a culturally accepted arrangement. But forget all of that. I am not claiming a spiritual sonship for myself only. All of you, too, are her sons spiritually. You became that when you were baptized."

"All right," Thaddeus responds, "I can see that."

"Me too," beams Simon the Zealot.

"Wow," exclaims Matthias. "You have very interesting and enlightening conversations in this Upper Room."

"Yes, we do," says Andrew with a chuckle.

---

[149] Mt 20:20-28

Matthew speaks next, very slowly, with grave solemnity. "So what we have here is the answer. We, brothers with Mary, the others, and Jesus, are the Archetype of the Ninth Blessing. I had thought all along that Jesus Himself would be that Archetype, or perhaps that Jesus and Mary would be that Archetype. After all, that mirrors the Archetypes of the First Blessing, who were also a man and a woman."

"Yes, Matthew, precisely," says John. "But, for this whole analogy to work, it can't be just Mary and Jesus because theirs is a Mother and Son relationship, not a Husband and Wife. However, when you add that we, too, and the many other disciples Jesus made these past three years and the many more that we are called to make by baptizing them in the name of the Father, Son, and Holy Spirit, all of these Sons and daughters with Mary comprise the Bride of Christ. This arrangement also fulfills one other mystery we find in Genesis. Ponder the meaning of these words. *I will put enmity between you and the woman, and between your offspring and hers; They will strike at your head, while you strike at their heel.* [150] Mary is that woman. We are her offspring. Together with Jesus, our brother, we are called to fight and conquer Satan."

The room becomes silent. They are stunned, filled with awe. Their minds are swirling. It's too much to comprehend, which applies to everyone, not just Matthew. They have lost track of time. It is early morning. They fasted and prayed and spoke words of truth to each other twenty-four more hours from sun rise to sun rise. The earth rotates on its axis another minute, bringing those

---

[150] Gn 3:15

assembled in the Upper Room face to face with the rising sun. The disciples, the mother of Jesus, and others have been there for ten days since Jesus' ascension when it happened.

Part Two

Spring, AD 30: fifty days after Jesus' resurrection, ten days after His ascension, early morning, Yom Rishon, the first day, in the Upper Room in Jerusalem, devoting themselves with one accord to prayer, together with some women and Mary the mother of Jesus and his brothers, receiving power from the Holy Spirit.

When the time for Pentecost was fulfilled, they were all in one place together. And suddenly there came from the sky a noise like a strong driving wind, and it filled the entire house in which they were. Then there appeared to them tongues as of fire, which parted and came to rest on each one of them. And they were all filled with the holy Spirit and began to speak in different tongues, as the Spirit enabled them to proclaim. [151]

Events move very quickly after the Holy Spirit's descent. Everyone in the Upper Room greets one another in a common language. The curse of the Tower of Babel is lifted. At nine o'clock, in response to the voices of doubters, those accusing the crowd of being drunk, Peter stands up and preaches boldly, explaining to a large crowd from all nations that everyone could hear and

---

[151] Acts 2:1-4

understand their words due to the Holy Spirit and the fulfillment of the Prophets.

James reminds them of Isaiah's words: *"In days to come, The mountain of the LORD's house shall be established as the highest mountain and raised above the hills. All nations shall stream toward it."* [152]

John reminds them of Joel's words. *"It shall come to pass. I will pour out my spirit upon all flesh. Your sons and daughters will prophesy, your old men will dream dreams, your young men will see visions. Even upon your male and female servants, in those days, I will pour out my spirit. I will set signs in the heavens and on the earth, blood, fire, and columns of smoke; The sun will darken, the moon turn blood-red, Before the day of the LORD arrives, that great and terrible day. Then everyone who calls upon the name of the LORD will escape harm. For on Mount Zion there will be a remnant, as the LORD has said, And in Jerusalem survivors whom the LORD will summon."* [153]

Matthew watches it all, not missing a detail, not worrying that he will forget. He feels and sees the Holy Spirit in some mysterious way. He thinks, did we just complete the First part, a universal greeting from us Apostles to the world?

Peter then stands and describes many things linking past events of Israel's history, prophecies, and the end times with Jesus Christ, the Davidic King, the Messiah, culminating with the words, *"Therefore let the whole house of Israel know for certain that*

---

[152] Isa 2:2
[153] Joel 3:1-5

*God has made him both Lord and Messiah, this **Jesus whom you crucified**."* [154]

Matthew heard the emphasis "***Jesus whom you crucified***" and was certain the crowd had too. He watches keenly as the next part of the scene unfolds. *"Now when they heard this, they were cut to the heart, and they asked Peter and the other apostles, "What are we to do, my brothers?" Peter [said] to them, "Repent and be baptized, every one of you, in the name of Jesus Christ for the forgiveness of your sins; and you will receive the gift of the holy Spirit."* [155] Matthew thinks, did we just complete the Second part, a universal confession?

Matthew watches keenly as the scene continues to unfold before his eyes. As many come forward to be baptized, Peter leads them in prayer, saying, *"Kyrie Eleison, Christe Eleison, Kyrie Eleison."* [156]

Immediately after completing this thrice-fold request for mercy, Peter leads everyone to praise God, singing, *"Glory to God in the highest, and on earth peace to people of good will. We praise you, we bless you, we adore you, we glorify you, we give you thanks for your great glory, Lord God, heavenly King, O God, almighty Father. Lord Jesus Christ, Only Begotten Son, Lord God, Lamb of God, Son of the Father, you take away the sins of the world, have mercy on us; you take away the sins of the world, receive our prayer; you are seated at the right hand of the Father, have mercy on us. For you alone are the Holy One, you alone are the Lord, you alone are the Most High, Jesus Christ, with the Holy Spirit, in the glory of God the Father. Amen."* [157]

---

[154] Acts 2:34 emphasis mine
[155] Acts 2:37-38
[156] The Kyrie as it is said in Mass
[157] The Gloria as it is said in Mass

Matthew counts Three and thinks they have confessed. They have praised God, confirming their belief in His power to change them. They are coming forward to be baptized and will receive the Holy Spirit fully.

Matthew listens intently as Peter *"testified with many other arguments, and was exhorting them, "Save yourselves from this corrupt generation."* He watches as *"those who accepted his message were baptized, and about three thousand persons were added that day."* [158]

He carefully catalogs Peter's words when *"testifying with many other arguments and was exhorting them."* There were readings from the Torah and the Psalms, and Peter explained many things. He led them in a summary statement of the fundamental beliefs of the Apostles and then a prayer, interceding for them, the local community, and the whole world.

When Peter finishes, Matthew counts Four and Five.

He watches. The room is aroar with joy. Matthew can no longer stay silent. He stands on a table and shouts, "Brothers and sisters, Jesus is here."

The room falls silent. Matthew repeats, "Jesus is here in Spirit. In a few moments, He will be here in flesh and blood."

Most of the new converts don't understand. They look at Matthew as if he has gone mad. None of them had any thought of Jesus as being among them, not in Spirit and most definitely not in the flesh. He was crucified and died. He rose from the dead and ascended to heaven to be with God. That's where Jesus is, as far as they understand. They had heard Peter's preaching

---

[158] Acts 2:40-41

and felt that the Holy Spirit was the answer, the entire answer to His mysterious presence among them, but they were wrong. They grasp and understand the Spirit's presence among them, but very few understand Matthew's words about Jesus. Only the twelve, Jesus' mother, and others who have followed Him, understand.

"He is here," Matthew repeats. "You must look with the eyes of faith." "Where is He? Did he come back again," some of them ask. Matthew continues. "Peter, you have greeted them, led them to confession, confirmed them, preached the Word of God, and led them in many prayers. We have completed the first five parts of this celebration. You have taught them *to devote themselves to the teaching of the apostles.* [159] Now, it is time to prepare them for the feast. The fast is over. They must learn to devote themselves *to the communal life, to the breaking of the bread and to the prayers.*" [160]

Immediately after Matthew says this, many new converts bring forth gifts, food, clothes, money, and other valuables. It takes some doing to get it all organized. Then Peter stands and motions his hands. A boy comes forward. Matthew winks at him. It is the same one Matthew encouraged a year back when Jesus fed the five thousand. This boy is well-versed in things of the altar. With a twinkle in his eye and a big smile, the boy presents some bread and a little leather pouch full of water.

Matthew watches the proceedings and keeps counting. Six and seven follow in rapid succession. Peter prepares the altar, prays over the gifts, asks God to accept them, and invites those present to pray that God would find the gifts acceptable - Six.

---

[159] Acts 2:42a
[160] Acts 2:42b

He instructs them to *"lift up their hearts,"* and they reply, *"We lift them up to the Lord"* [161] – Matthew says "Six" as the sixth Beatitude rushes into his mind, *"Blessed are the clean of heart for they shall see God.* [162] Oh, yes, they and we shall see God in just a few moments."

Peter then leads them to sing *"Holy, Holy, Holy Lord God of hosts. Heaven and earth are full of your glory. Hosanna in the highest. Blessed is he who comes in the name of the Lord, Hosanna in the highest."* [163] – Matthew shouts, "Seven, this is your hour of Glory, Son of David."

Matthew watches the proceedings and keeps counting. As all pray the Lord's Prayer together, Matthew counts, but starts at One again: *'Our Father in heaven,"* One; *"hallowed be your name,"* Two; *"your kingdom come your will be done on earth as it is in heaven,"* Three; *"give us this day our daily bread,"* Four; *"and forgive us our trespasses as we forgive those who trespass against us,"* Five' *"and lead us not into temptation,"* Six; *"but deliver us from evil,"* [164] - Seven.

At this point, everyone stops praying except Peter. Matthew thinks eight comes after seven and listens as Peter prays, *"Deliver us, Lord, we pray, from every evil, graciously grant peace in our days, that, by the help of your mercy, we may be always free from sin and safe from all distress, as we await the blessed hope and the coming of our Savior, Jesus Christ."* [165]

---

[161] As it is prayed in every Mass
[162] The Sixth Beatitude, Matthew 5:8
[163] As it is prayed in every Mass
[164] The first seven parts of the Our Father as they are prayed in every Mass.
[165] The embolism as it is prayed in Mass

Peter stops and waits. He is waiting for the participants to answer. Matthew thinks nine comes after eight and remembers the words Jesus had taught them. "Listen to me, and repeat what I say," he shouts to all present. *"For thine is the kingdom and the power and the glory, now and forever, Amen."* [166] Everyone repeats the words, and Matthew counts Nine.

After a few more prayers and a peaceful greeting, Peter holds up the consecrated host and says, *"Behold the Lamb of God, behold Him who takes away the sins of the world. Blessed are those called to the Supper of the Lamb."* [167] Peter does the same with the wine. Matthew silently counts – Nine, again. He thinks again; nine comes after eight. We are in the ninth part of this ceremony.

Everyone comes forward to receive the Lord. They hear Peter and the other eleven say, *"The body of Christ and the blood of Christ,"* and respond, *"Amen."* [168] And then, *"Their eyes were opened when they ate the bread."* [169] Yes, that is correct- their eyes were opened after they ate the bread. They knew by faith that He was with them and, even better, in them. Nine, again, Matthew counts.

The boy adamantly insists it was water in the pouch, but everyone present said it was the choicest of wines. The boy says he brought only enough bread and wine for perhaps twenty persons, but they feed over three thousand. Peter dismisses everyone and encourages all to go out into the world to proclaim the gospel.

---

[166] The Doxology as it is prayed in every Mass
[167] As the words are said in every Mass
[168] As the words are said in every Mass
[169] Lk 24:31

Matthew thinks the end returns to the beginning again. He counts One.

Later that evening, Matthew contemplates and counts with John. He says, "Nine Blessings, Nine Mountains, Nine Archetypes representing Nine eras, Nine parts to the Prayer, Nine words on the cross, Nine parts to the New Covenant Passover. I have two questions, John. Did He give us Seven Sacraments or Nine? That's the first question. Listen to my second question. We agree that this First Revelation of the Nine Part ceremony has nine parts. However, when I consider, when I count and contemplate what we will be doing every time we celebrate like this when we literally bring Heaven to Earth and establish His kingdom: when I consider all of this and more, I know in my heart of hearts, something profound is happening. But being the earthly focused counting contemplative I am, I know I won't have the spiritual insight required to describe what is happening for the world to see."

John thinks for a moment and says, "Let's pray about it, Matthew. Perhaps God will provide a deeper revelation so that we might learn to appreciate the profundities of which you speak."

Matthew says, "I like that idea, John."

CHAPTER 11

CONTEMPLATING A VISION OF THE HEAVENLY CITY USING THE RULE OF SEVENS AND TWELVES

One of the seven angels who held the seven bowls filled with the seven last plagues came and said to me, "Come here. I will show you the bride, the wife of the Lamb." He took me in spirit to a great, high mountain and showed me the holy city Jerusalem coming down out of heaven from God. It gleamed with the splendor of God. Its radiance was like that of a precious stone, like jasper, clear as crystal. It had a massive, high wall, with twelve gates where twelve angels were stationed and on which names were inscribed, [the names] of the twelve tribes of the Israelites. There were three gates facing east, three north, three south, and three west. The wall of the city had twelve courses of stones as its foundation, on which were inscribed the twelve names of the twelve apostles of the Lamb. [170]

---

[170] Rev 21:9-14

Spring, circa AD 95: sunrise, the first day or the eighth day, Sunday, about sixty years after Jesus ascended, on Mount Profitis Ilias on the Island of Patmos in the Aegean Sea, elevation 260 meters above sea level, in the region of modern-day Grand Royal Basilica in honor of Saint John, modern-day Turkey, formerly of the Ottoman Empire, formerly of the Seljuk Empire, formerly of the Byzantine Empire, formerly of the Roman Empire under the rule of Emperor Domitian.

Part One

The day starts like many others, welcomed by bright sunshine, a clear sky, and cool air. The aromatic flora—sage, thyme, and oregano—pleasantly saturates John's mood, filling him with hope. He is sitting in an olive grove, contemplating events in another Olive Grove about sixty years ago. So much has happened since then. He misses his friends, Jesus, and His disciples. He misses Mary, his mother.

He admires the anemones, poppies, and other wildflowers colorfully splashed about, and he thinks of Matthew. "You would have loved to live here, dear Brother. How about this, Matthew, for punishment? I think you would have welcomed this kind of punishment." A pang pierces his heart when he recalls how Matthew died, martyred cruelly, like the other ten and many others daring to profess Jesus as Lord.

He gets up and starts the forty-minute hike down to the Aegean Sea, where he will bathe to prepare himself for the liturgy. The small game perks up as he passes, but none scurries away. They know him well. He has been here for over a year, living alone in exile because of His testimony of Jesus Christ.

He removes his sandals and garments, strolls across a warm stretch of sand, and silently slides into the crystal-clear water, trying to minimize any disturbance of the aquatic life. Today, his efforts pay off. A school of bogues swims past, not more than ten feet in front of him, their silvery bodies and greenish tint reflecting before him. As the last of them swim past, an octopus, about a meter in length, comes into view. It lulls about calmly, not bothering to change its color or do anything else that might signify fear. It, too, knows John. "Hello there, my Lady of Eights. My friend Matthew would have envied you, having eight to write with." He spots a few red pandas and thinks of the meal they could make. "No need to worry today, my fishy fellas. Today is my day of rest, so let it be that way for you also."

He swims 100 meters along the shoreline in a westerly direction to a small pool in an alcove, where he finds some clay and plants that he grinds together in his hands to make a soapy substance to wash with. He doesn't wash his body on the Lord's Day to purify himself before worship. Jesus taught them to clean what's on the inside. No, he washes because it is his routine. Even though he will see no one else, he does it. Solitary living is smoother if it includes some routines. It provides a sense of time. Yes, the celestial elements mark the seasons and provide a natural rhythm to life. Still, personal routines do the same but in a more personal way. They help a man keep track of and organize his life, with its schedules and events, and whatever else should not be forgotten-which is the other reason he washes, to remind himself what needs washing on his inside. And, what better time than now, immediately before worshipping on the Lord's Day?

He thinks to himself, "I don't need to be forgiven for that sin again, but it still clings to me and must be washed from my conscience, repeatedly, until the Lord, in His mercy, removes even its memory. Until then, I will never forget that moment. It was a decision made in a moment, but that moment revealed much," he says out loud. "Nor should I forget that moment."

He is just getting out of the water and putting his garments back on. "Adam and Eve, who feared death, sinned and were given garments. Tamar used Judah's cord and seal to get what she wanted and succeeded because he had sinned and feared the scorching death he prescribed for her. Potiphar's wife stole Joseph's garment and did not get what she wanted because he had not sinned, trusted God, and did not fear death. I ran that night, Lord, in haste because I feared death. Fearing death, I lost my outer cover, but more importantly, I fled from the interior garment of a clean conscience." Putting his sandals on, he pauses to let the confession settle in and wash his conscience.

He starts the spoken monologue again. "You forgave me the next time our eyes met. You said, *"Behold your mother."* I looked into her eyes and saw forgiveness. I saw, too, the path of penance. Loving her was, is, and always will be my expression of gratitude, just like loving you in this Eucharistic celebration will forever be my expression of gratitude."

Having further cleaned his inside, he heads up the mountain to prepare for the next routine he will never forget, the Liturgy. He doesn't need anyone or anything to remind him of that. Grinding the wheat and grapes, he routinely works to ensure a ready stash of the two essential elements is available- these routines are ensconced in his person. "Routines are good," he reminds himself. Little did he know that this day would be anything but routine.

About an hour later, he holds a small piece of bread and a small cup of wine. He has finished the Liturgy of the Word, not leaving out one word or detail of what the Lord had taught them. He offers the bread and wine, says the prayer of consecration, and then it happens, and what happened is dramatic. John had seen, heard, and experienced much during his days with Jesus. He had said more than once and even written in his Gospel, *"There are also many other things that Jesus did, but if these were to be described individually, I do not think the whole world would contain the books that would be written."* [171]

Still, what he saw, heard, and experienced on this day on the Island of Patmos is far beyond everything he experienced previously compared to it. He described the vision starting as thus:

The Beginning of the Book of Revelation

"The revelation of Jesus Christ, which God gave to him, to show his servants what must happen soon. He made it known by sending his angel to his servant John, who gives witness to the word of God and to the testimony of Jesus Christ by reporting what he saw.

Blessed is the one who reads aloud and blessed are those who listen to this prophetic message and heed what is written in it, for the appointed time is near." [172]

---

[171] Jn 21:25
[172] Rev 1:1-3

Part Two

He writes *Revelation* over several months, waiting on the Holy Spirit as he has learned to do and writing what is brought to his mind. He spends much time contemplating what he has seen and heard on this mountain. He compares and contrasts the shocking heavenly vision with many prior experiences over the past sixty years, especially what he and Matthew called the First Revelation of the Ninth Archetype, the Tenth Mountaintop Experience.

The disciples witnessed and participated in that celebration led by the Son of David on the mountain of David's Jerusalem. In response to Mathew's question on that day, John suggested they think for a moment and pray. He wondered aloud if God would provide a deeper revelation so that they might learn to appreciate the profundities of which Mathew spoke. At some point, as did all twelve Apostles, they parted ways to travel to a place directed by the Holy Spirit to proclaim the Gospel. John had learned that he was the last remaining Apostle.

His mother, too, had passed on. Many had thought her manner of departure strange, for she had left no trace of her death. The early Christians always collected and preserved the remains of these earliest martyrs of the Church. They venerated their bones and often built an altar and then a church over the spot where they fell. But no one found a trace of Mary's body. John thinks he knows what happened. He believes his mother was assumed into heaven. It makes perfect sense that God, Jesus, would prevent her body from seeing decay. The body of she who carried divinity, body, and soul in her body; her body must never experience decay.

Leaving his contemplations of Mary, John's thoughts turn to Matthew again.

"Matthew, you should have seen what I saw here. You would have expected this final revelation to showcase the number nine, but that was not what I saw and heard."

"Really, John, please tell me what you saw." He imagines Matthew saying that. He has picked up Matthew's habit of having lengthy conversations with himself.

"I think I can be justified in doing this," he playfully says out loud, as if Matthew was right next to him listening.

He continues. "Seven is the number of focus right from the beginning throughout the entire vision right to its end. We have seven Churches, seven Spirits, Golden lampstands, stars, seals, horns and eyes, angels and trumpets."

"And don't forget the seven thunders, the seven thousand people killed in an earthquake, or the seven heads, crowns plagues, golden bowls, hills, and kings." He imagines Matthew giving this long list of sevens with a flourish.

He imagines Matthew's reaction when he says with a greater flourish, "And my dear Matthew, let's not forget the seven Blessings He spoke."

John continues before the imaginary Matthew can respond to the ever-so-small slight. "I am sure, Matthew, you would have noted the other numbers, such as three, four, one thousand, fifteen hundred, six hundred-sixty-six, and twelve. You are an observant fellow. And you would agree that none comes close to being presented so prominently and consistently as seven. Still, Matthew, I bet you will see the wisdom as soon as you step back to contemplate the whole story of God's Revelation. Genesis cannot be clearer. God created the universe in six days and then took another day, the seventh, to establish humanity's special purpose, to rest with Him."

The imaginary Matthew, got a word in. "Yes, the Beatitudes have this way of returning to things. The eighth returns to the first. Now, God's plan brings humanity back to seven, a special relationship with Him as it was at first."

"Bravo, Matthew. Have you moved on from your nonuple of ideas, theories, events, sequences, people, archetypes, blessings, and mountains?"

"Not so fast," says imaginary Matthew. Everything has its' time and place, and you, my friend, speak of the eternal. My rule of nines did and now does apply to earthly things, especially those concerned with bringing earthly things to heavenly ends."

Part Three

At some point, John can't exactly recall; he realizes that his imaginary conversation with an imaginary Matthew is not, in truth, imaginary. Rather, it is prayer. His posture says the same. He is kneeling- this explains why the conversations progress so much faster on the Lord's Day, or more precisely, during the celebration of the liturgy.

"It's called the Communion of Saints," he imagines; no, he hears Matthew say one day.

"John, I am not surprised by the sevens focus. Nor am I surprised by Revelation's focus on twelves as it approaches its end."

"Matthew," John prays. I imagine you would have also understood the significance of the other numbers. I imagine that had you been here on earth counting and contemplating with me, we would have been pleasantly surprised by the sudden prominent appearance of twelve at the end of this *Revelation*."

"Dear Matthew," John continues, "Would you ever have imagined that we would be portrayed as the foundation? Let me remind you of what He said. *"The wall of the city had twelve courses of stones as its foundation, on which were inscribed the twelve names of the twelve apostles of the Lamb."* [173]

"Why do you find it hard to believe this, John? Think again about the Genesis creation account. While it does not explicitly mention a twelve-month year, it does contain imagery related to the creation of time and seasons. [174] We read how God created the lights in the sky (the sun, moon, and stars) to separate day from night and to serve as signs for seasons, days, and years. Learning from God's example of counting seven days to define one week, humanity started counting twelve months to define one year. Our ancestors observed the moon and the stars and created a calendar based on the twelve cycles the moon takes in one year. Thus, the numbers seven and twelve define human history, especially its history with God, its creator. God's *Revelation* has confirmed that this pattern did not change."

John marveled at Matthew's wisdom, the once over perseverating detail guy now seeing the big picture with remarkable clarity. "I look forward to the day when we can speak face to face again, Matthew."

---

[173] Rev 21:14
[174] Gn 1:14-18

Matthew continued. "John, let me remind you we are far more than what you spoke a moment ago. We are far more than a mere portrayal of the Eternal City's foundation. We are the City's foundation."

"Matthew," John marvels. "Your spiritual insights are soaring."

"Yes, John- that's because I am in the presence of unalloyed glory."

"Still, Matthew," John responds with a twinge of sadness. I ran that night. My abandonment of the Lord in His hour of greatest need carries a greater guilt because I was the one he loved especially. Why should my name appear on that Foundation? Furthermore, I have not been martyred like the rest of you."

"You are suffering for your testimony, John. Our Lord is pleased. You are walking with him, loving him and us, his Body, Bride, and Church."

The words flow over John, saturating his thirsty soul. So enraptured is he in prayer that he sees Matthew and so too, the others with Jesus and His Mother, Mary, all of them smiling at him. He bows low to the ground, touching his face to the fresh grass. "Thank you. Thank you all for this encouragement. I am prepared to move on. The Mass is ended. I will go in peace."

Part Four

Later that day, John is conversing with Matthew again. "Matthew, we must answer this question of the location of this New Jerusalem. The old one has been sacked and burned to the ground. No stone in the Temple is lying on top of another, just as Our Lord predicted. The same is true of most of its buildings. Meanwhile,

I am alone on this island, celebrating the Lord's Passover. Others are scattered about the known world doing the same. Is it true that the New Jerusalem is Rome?"

"Yes, John, that is correct. Because of its strategic importance, it is the logical place for the Church to gather and focus its Apostolic succession."

"I guess it's no accident, Matthew, that Peter and Paul, two pillars of the Church, were martyred in Rome."

"Yes, John, their bones will find a place under the altar of a Church we will build there. Many more martyrs will follow. That's good news, John."

"Did I hear you say, 'Good News,' Matthew? Perhaps this explains something else I saw in the vision."

"Please explain, John."

John pauses to collect himself. He wants to ensure he says it right. "I saw something else incredible in my vision on the Lord's Day." He stops and looks at Matthew.

"What did you see, John?"

"I saw the Ark of the Covenant."

Beaming with joy, Matthew exclaims, "Of course you did! You saw *the Woman, the Ark of the Covenant, the one clothed with the sun, with the moon under her feet, and on her head a crown of twelve stars?*" [175]

"Yes, Matthew, that's the *Woman* I saw, and we know from Jericho what happens when the Ark of the Covenant is in front of the armies of God leading the way. Please give her my greetings."

---

[175] Rev 11:19-12:1

"John, I do not need to greet her for you. Every word you speak and pray passes through her to Jesus, her Son. She hears it and brings it to Him again and again."

"I saw something else, Matthew."

"Please tell me, John, what you saw."

"A prolonged silence follows. John feels tears welling in his eyes. They are tears of joy. He has felt this way before, the heavy, weighty, loving closeness of His God, the Father, Son, and Holy Spirit."

"Yes, Matthew, let me describe the rest of what I saw. *She was with child and wailed aloud in pain as she labored to give birth. Then another sign appeared in the sky; it was a huge red dragon, with seven heads and ten horns, and on its heads were seven diadems. Its tail swept away a third of the stars in the sky and hurled them down to the earth. Then the dragon stood before the woman about to give birth, to devour her child when she gave birth. She gave birth to a son, a male child, destined to rule all the nations with an iron rod. Her child was caught up to God and his throne. The woman herself fled into the desert where she had a place prepared by God, that there she might be taken care of for twelve hundred and sixty days. Then war broke out in heaven; Michael and his angels battled against the dragon. The dragon and its angels fought back, but they did not prevail and there was no longer any place for them in heaven. The huge dragon, the ancient serpent, who is called the Devil and Satan, who deceived the whole world, was thrown down to earth, and its angels were thrown down with it.*" [176]

---

[176] Rev 12:2-9

"John, that's the Gospel. That's the Good News."

"Yes, Matthew, I heard Him say this. *They conquered him by the blood of the Lamb and by the word of their testimony; love for life did not deter them from death.*" [177]

"Amen, John, what else did you expect!"

"Amen, Matthew."

"Amen and Amen," both disciples say to close the conversation.

---

[177] Rev 12:11

CHAPTER 12

BUILDING MY HOUSE USING THE RULE OF NINES

Everyone who listens to these words of mine and acts on them will be like a wise man who built his house on rock. The rain fell, the floods came, and the winds blew and buffeted the house. But it did not collapse; it had been set solidly on rock. And everyone who listens to these words of mine but does not act on them will be like a fool who built his house on sand. The rain fell, the floods came, and the winds blew and buffeted the house. And it collapsed and was completely ruined. When Jesus finished these words, the crowds were astonished at his teaching, for he taught them as one having authority, and not as their scribes. [178]

---

[178] Mt 7:24-29

About twenty centuries later, AD 2024: All Saints Day, November 1st - Reverend Father William C. Forrey, the Fifth Ruling Pastor of the Holy Name of Jesus Church Harrisburg, Pennsylvania, Ruled by Most Reverend Father Timothy C. Senior, the Twelfth Bishop of Harrisburg, Ruled by Pope Francis, the 266th Bishop of Rome, Vicar of Jesus Christ, Successor of the Prince of the Apostles, Supreme Pontiff of the Universal Church, Primate of Italy, Archbishop and Metropolitan of the Roman Province, Sovereign of the Vatican City State, Servant of the Servants of God.

Building good earthly cities starts with building good earthly houses. Every earthly city includes many earthly houses. Good earthly city planners design, organize, and construct the city's infrastructure to serve the common good: the people who live in its many houses.

Building glorious heavenly cities starts with building glorious heavenly people. God's heavenly city includes many heavenly people. God builds houses with love, which fit into His grand plan to build a glorious and eternal city.

I have written this book to encourage Christians of all denominations and states in life, whether married, single, or consecrated, to consider how they can and why they should cooperate with God to build a house that can withstand the evils, the rain, floods, and winds of their generation.

With the last words of the Sermon on the Mount, Jesus has done many things, a few of which I want to consider now. First, Jesus used the analogy of building a house to convey that everyone is building something in the very process of living.

Some are building houses that will last. Others are building houses that will not last, but in either case, everyone is building whether or not they realize it. Secondly, Jesus has called us to contemplate the words of the Sermon on the Mount to build our house, starting with the one hundred-twenty words and nine sentences the Church calls the Beatitudes and finishing with the two thousand one hundred-nineteen words that follow. Thirdly, he didn't say count as you build, but I believe he wants us to count as we contemplate how to build our lives so that they may please God.

What does building a life that pleases God mean? It means striving to please God in everything. It means striving to know and do his will in every aspect of our lives, meaning our actions, words, thoughts, prayers, contemplations, and counts.

Still, there are many things in life to do, say, think, pray, contemplate, and count, so building a life that pleases God may feel overwhelming, and, frankly, the idea of counting to find God may feel incredibly boring. But if we start where Jesus started, we can count and contemplate laser-like on the nine most important ideas for completing and creating the life God has planned for us. We can use the architectural blueprint (note here we speak not of archetypal) He left us. This blueprint has nine parts. In this chapter, I want to share an abbreviated version of the house I am building based on the Rule of Nines. [179] Mind you, it is evolving.

---

[179] The Rule of Nines is a method of assessing the size and thus the severity of a burn that I learned during my general surgical training. It allowed us to quickly estimate the total body surface area (TBSA) affected by

Some of my Counts and Contemplations

"One, two, three, four, five, six, seven, eight, nine! I landed on free parking, Pop! You don't stand a chance now." My six-year-old grandson was defeating me handily in a third Monopoly game in one morning. He chuckled as his nine-year-old brother, serving as the banker, counted what he had just inherited. "One $500 bill, two $100 bills, three $50s, four $20s, five $10s, six $5s, and seven $1s: Hum, that adds up to $1017." Checking his quick mental calculations on my phone calculator twice, I moaned and asked to concede the game, but they would hear of no such thing.

Like my grandsons, I did a lot of counting as a young boy, mostly for fun. One day, after counting the thirty or so trees in my yard, my friend and I decided to climb every tree. I am not certain what exactly motivated us to climb them all, but I have an idea. In the first place, we thought it would be fun, and we had restless energy in our legs and arms. Secondly, the trees waited patiently, joyfully expecting us to climb them. I should clarify that we had certainly climbed them, all of them, many times before that day. Thirdly, and I think this is the real reason we counted the trees, counting them put them in a new context. Instead of being just

---

burns. This estimation is crucial for guiding treatment decisions, such as fluid resuscitation. The Rule of Nines divides the body into sections, each representing approximately 9% (or multiples of 9%) of the TBSA: Head and Neck: 9%, Each Arm: 9% (front and back combined), Each Leg: 18% (front and back combined), Anterior Torso: 18%, Posterior Torso: 18%, Perineum: 1%. This method allows for a rapid and straightforward assessment, which is particularly useful in emergency situations.

individual trees, all of them were part of one group of trees, and we wanted to establish our dominion, as it were, over that group.

I also did a lot of counting as a young boy between the fourth and eighth grades when I was bored in a car for about an hour per day, five days per week, riding to and from my child psychoanalyst's office. The restless energy in my legs and arms craved free expression, and the world outside the car beckoned. Given that I couldn't join it, I observed it. I played counting games. One of my favorites is a game I now call the mathematical reduction to zero game. The game started when I noticed numbers outside the car, usually on a sign or a license plate. Let's say that I saw the number 3471. I would make the following mental calculations. 3 plus 4 equals 7. 7 divided by 7 equals 1. 1 minus 1 equals 0. In this instance, reaching zero was simple, requiring just three calculations. However, I encountered other numbers requiring more mental gymnastics. Let's think about 5886. 5 times 8 equals 40. 4 plus 0 equals 4. 4 times 8 equals 32. 3 times 2 equals 6. 6 minus 6 equals 0. That game took five calculations. Let's try one more, this time with five numbers, 72854. 7 times 2 equals 14. I can express the 1 in 14 as 1 divided by 1 or 1/1. Then, I can add 1 plus 1 to get a second 2 and multiply it by the new 4 to get 8. I add the new 8 to the first 8 to get 16. Expressing the 1 in 16 again as 1/1, I again have two 1s with which to work. I subtract the first 1 from 6 to get 5 and add the second 1 to 4 to make 5. 5 minus 5 equals 0. I used nine steps in this mathematical reduction to zero game from start to finish, all done mentally without counting on my fingers.

I want to make some observations about this game to anticipate your questions. First, the rule allowing me to express one as 1/1 gives me a great advantage, especially considering the second rule of the game, which stipulated that I could make that calculation twice in each game. Now, I could easily convert one 1 into four 1s, each of which I could add, subtract, divide, or multiply by the other numbers. With these two rules, the possibilities of number gymnastics become infinite, limited only by the capacity of my mind to juggle them around.

My second observation is that I have no ill feelings about creating a game with rules ensuring my success. Nor will I entertain the skeptics who want to poke holes in my game. Remember, my dear reader, the game flowed from the mind of a bored, restless adolescent boy feeling cooped up in a car and heading to and from an appointment with his psychoanalyst. Do you want to deny that boy a bit of liberty? Of course, the reason for describing my counting games has little to do with obtaining your approval. Rather, I am providing context to a major theme of my life- I like to count things, people, places, words, expressions, biblical verses, and just about anything, place, time, or purpose. It is my love for counting which draws me to Matthew.

Saint Matthew, the author of the Gospel, which contains the fullest version of Christ's most famous sermon, the Sermon on the Mount, was a tax collector, so he had to be very good at playing counting games. He was known for cheating tax-paying relatives and less educated publicans, which, I bet, he accomplished by tricking them with counting games. Fortunately, Matthew gave up the practice of dishonest counting after he met Jesus, but this does not mean that Matthew gave up thinking mathematically. I have a hunch that counting, organizing, and representing numbers symbolically and other counting-related thought processes filled

Matthew's mind. I bet Matthew asked numerically related questions when reading scrolls, especially the Torah.

Like Matthew, I, too, switched from counting for fun and admittedly cheating people to counting to understand God, be it in His revealed word, the Bible, or my life, what God reveals to me through the events, circumstances, and people of my life. To be clear, I still count for fun. That Monopoly game took place just a few years ago. I hope to play many more counting games with my grandchildren because counting games such as Monopoly, Life, and Battleship facilitate life lessons and perhaps instill the idea of counting as a way to search for God. They also instill the idea that finding God and learning life lessons can and should be fun. I like to read stories with grandchildren for the same reasons. I think 'Once upon a time' and 'They lived happily ever after' provide an ideal construct for teaching life lessons and teaching that reading should be done for a good purpose.

Counting whatever, whenever, and however, I did it in the past has meant something different to me over various phases of my life. In high school, I counted how many friends I had. When did I count them?- far too often. How did I count them?; I suspect my criteria were not very sound measures of true friendship. Let's leave it at that. In college, I still counted friends, again too often, and used poor criteria. I also counted the points I would need on various tests to get a good grade in class. During my medical school years, I counted less of the first and more of the second and started counting a third thing, the number of days until graduation. During the seven years of my general surgery training, what I counted were the years, months, weeks, days, and hours until graduating from that arduous journey. I did this more often the further along in training I progressed. I also counted and recorded the number of cases I did.

It wasn't until after my life took a dramatic turn in a direction I hadn't planned that I started counting spiritual things. The dramatic change occurred twelve years after I finished my surgical residency. Being twelve years into the practice of general surgery, I was twenty-nine years into learning, planning, preparing, and practicing the art I had planned to retire doing. I turned forty-five years old on the day that the change started. It was a difficult time for my wife of twenty-two years and my four children, ages twenty-one, eighteen, fifteen, and ten at the time.

In addition to changing how I counted, meaning spiritually, God worked in me to change when, where, what, and why I counted. He did this in January 2014 by prompting me to memorize chapters five, six, and seven of Matthew's Gospel, the Sermon on the Mount.

As I pondered the Sermon's first nine sentences, counting spiritually facilitated my journey toward God. Counting the Beatitudes seemed easy to me. Many Christian authors speak of six, seven, or eight Beatitudes. I simply counted the number of times Jesus said, *"Blessed are,"* to start a sentence. He said that nine times and so nine would become the lens through which I thought, analyzed, and prayed over the rest of the Sermon on the Mount. Over time, the rule of nines became a guiding concept for my approach to the entire Bible and so too, as a Catholic, to God's other divinely revealed truths, the sacred Traditions preserved by the Catholic Church. Lastly, it became a guiding concept for how I live.

How I count spiritually stems directly from the Beatitudes. It's not that nine is a magical number. It's that Jesus Christ is portrayed in the Bible as starting His three-year ministry with nine blessings. Looking at my life, I can see where God has revealed various truths of the Beatitudes, all nine, through my life experiences.

Let's briefly ponder the first blessing and how it became my first lesson in spiritual counting. It started with me being a patient. The year was 2002. Making me a patient, God flipped my life upside down. I was used to being the doctor, the one in charge, the one with answers to life's problems. Now, I was the one looking at others for answers. The experience lasted fifty days. It was an extended lesson in humility, something the proud surgeon desperately needed to learn. It reinvigorated my understanding of baptism. I learned to see my baptism, my regeneration as a child of God, as the essential core of my personhood. My status as a child of God precedes everything else. I am many things, a husband, father, friend, coworker, and surgeon, but none of this means anything unless it is based on a foundation of baptism and choosing to know, understand, and live as a child of God.

Not only this, but Jesus has taught me how to pray to understand my baptism more fully. When I pray, *"Our Father in heaven,"* I am reminded of two things. When I say *Our*, I am reminded that finding God must involve communion with other children of God. When I say *Father*, I am reminded of my baptism, of my status as a child of God, and my need to be poor in spirit.

Following the experience in which I learned to appreciate my baptism more fully, God led me through seven more distinct life experiences, each related to a Beatitude in the order that Jesus spoke them. I also learned to appreciate a corresponding portion of the Lord's Prayer and a sacrament, but this lengthy story is the topic of another book.

In concluding this book, I want to say that the process has started again. Yes, the eighth has met the first again. After being diagnosed with cancer in July 2024 and returning to being a patient a second time instead of the doctor, I see now that I have returned to the first Beatitude. Not surprisingly, I have much to learn about the first Beatitude. I suspect it is the same with everyone. We need spiritual lessons repeated if we want to learn them deeply.

Being a patient forced me once again to be dependent. Good patients are like children, humbly trusting the doctor to do something for them that they cannot do for themselves. They should be *"poor in spirit."* I thank God for my surgeon. He is competent, and God used him to remove a deadly disease when I was fast asleep, not even breathing. That's how dependent I became this past summer. Fortunately, it seems all of the cancer was removed before it had a chance to spread. I am looking forward to many more years, God willing. Still, I am also looking for and will continue counting and looking for more Beatitude lessons as I draw closer to God.

Regardless of where the cancer in my body leads me in terms of surgeons, doctor's offices, and hospitals, I will have missed its most important lesson if I fail to follow where it leads spiritually. I have cancer in my soul. Jesus said, *"Those who are healthy do not need a physician, but the sick do. I have not come to call the righteous to repentance but sinners."* [180] Doctor Luke, Matthew, and Mark captured these words, so I need to heed them.

How, When, Where, What and Why of Spiritual Counting

I want to unpack this idea of spiritual counting because I believe it will help us understand better our part as individuals in His plan to create something of tremendous glory. Yes, we play a small part individually in the grand scheme, yet each individual's small part has infinite value. We count and contemplate our blessings and failures to learn how to improve. We cooperate with God in His plan to build us into holy persons. We grow in holiness with God's help, but we must play our part.

Choosing freely to cooperate with God- that's **how** we grow. We must realize that God's time to grow in holiness is always now and will be forever- that's **when** we grow. God's primary place for this growth is in our hearts- that's **where** we grow. Spiritual growth and living is not natural, even after our baptism. We still live in a body and a world corrupted by evil- that's **what** we fight in order to grow.

What about why we fight? Why do we count and contemplate this journey so we can grow in holiness? What is our end purpose? We must ask this question, or this book serves no real purpose. We must ask this question or our life serves no real purpose. Even

---

[180] Lk 5:31-32, Mk 2:17, Mt 9:12-13

the atheist realized this. [181] Let's take a moment to consider the question in the context of this book.

We have taken an imaginary journey with Jesus and his twelve disciples. We imagined what they may have counted during and immediately after His three-year ministry with them. We counted the mountains they climbed and the biblical heroes they may have considered perfect models of significant salvation-history events. We call these people Archetypes of Blessings, the First, Second, and so on until we reach the Ninth. They serve as role models for beatific living. They guide us on spiritual counting.

We base our counting on the number of times Jesus said *"Blessed are"* as He started the most famous sermon ever preached, The Sermon on the Mount. He taught us how to count by teaching us the rule of nines. We started counting and contemplating where Jesus started.

Now, we must answer the question of why we count. To do so, we must end our contemplations where Jesus ended that Sermon- this is where we go to understand why He gave it in the first place. We must contemplate the very last words of the Sermon on the Mount.

"Everyone who listens to these words of mine and acts on them will be like a wise man who built his house on rock. The rain fell, the floods came, and the winds blew and buffeted the house. But it did not collapse; it had been set solidly on rock. And everyone who listens to these words of mine but does not act on them will be like a fool who built his house on sand. The rain fell, the floods came, and the winds

---

[181] Camus, Albert. The Myth of Sisyphus. Translated by Justin O'Brien, Vintage Books, 1991

blew and buffeted the house. And it collapsed and was completely ruined." [182]

We count because it directs our contemplation of God and His plans for us individually. More than this, these words call us to count and contemplate while listening actively and doing, at times, what is humanly impossible, like Noah. We must count in this way carefully and continually, for they provide a summary of Godly wisdom from the Lord Himself and a call to act. More still. He didn't leave us alone to do His will. He promised to be with us always, even unto the end of the age. He has done that in His Church and through the revelations He bestowed on her since then. He does it in scripture. He does it in orally preserved divine traditions. He does it with the laity, and He does it through the priesthood. Still, no matter how, when, where, what, and why this Church is being built, Jesus Christ is building it. He does it in the Church's worship, the Mass, where His people live with, through, and in Him.

We have considered the nine Archetypes of His nine Blessings as special role models who teach us how to build a Godly house by modeling God's truths. Now, we consider the Architectural Blueprint Jesus provided for us. One letter is changed, the fifth from 'e' to 'i.' Jesus' analogy isn't hard to understand. He characterizes His Sermon on the Mount as a literary Architectural Blueprint by which humans can build houses. Take some time now to use His blueprint as we count our days, contemplate His words, and act through, with, and in Him in the Sacraments He provides so that each of us might build a house that can find a place in His eternal city.

---

[182] Mt 7:24-27

EPILOGUE

CONTEMPLATING THE NINE BLESSINGS

The First Blessing

Blessed are the poor in Spirit, for theirs is the kingdom of heaven.

1. What does the first blessing mean to me; what does it mean for the Church?
2. What does praying *"Our Father in heaven"* teach me; what does it teach the Church about the first blessing?
3. How do Adam and Eve model the first blessing?
4. Am I a proud person?
5. Would my family and friends say I am a humble person?
6. Lord, when I pray, *"Our Father,"* please remind me of my Baptism and adoption into your family as a child of God and teach me to grow in humility.

The Second Blessing

Blessed are they who mourn, for they will be comforted.

1. What does the second blessing mean to me; what does it mean for the Church?
2. What does praying *"Hallowed be thy name"* teach me; what does it teach the Church about the second blessing?
3. How did Abel model the second blessing?
4. How often do I mourn my sin?
5. How often do I commit the same sin?
6. Do I make excuses for, minimize, and rationalize my sin?
7. Lord, grant me a sorrowful spirit quickly after I sin.
8. Lord, grant me a persistently sorrowful spirit until I rightly confess my sins.
9. Lord, when I pray *"Hallowed be thy name,"* let it remind me to praise you for comforting me every time you forgive my sins in the Sacrament of Reconciliation.

The Third Blessing

Blessed are the meek, for they will inherit the earth.

1. What does the third blessing mean to me; what does it mean for the Church?
2. What does praying *"Thy kingdom come, thy will be done on earth as it is in heaven"* teach me; what does it teach the Church about the third blessing?
3. How did Noah model the third blessing?
4. How many times has God asked me to do something that seems humanly impossible?
5. When God asks me to do something humanly impossible, do I depend on God or make excuses and find reasons to ignore his request?
6. Lord, help me respond better the next time you ask me to do something humanly impossible by meekly depending on you and the Holy Spirit with whom you empower me through the Sacrament of Confirmation.

The Fourth Blessing

Blessed are they who hunger and thirst for righteousness, for they shall be satisfied.

1. What does the fourth blessing mean to me; what does it mean for the Church?
2. What does praying *"Give us this day our daily bread"* teach me; what does it teach the Church about the fourth blessing?
3. How did Abraham model the fourth blessing?
4. How many times has my desire for righteousness caused me hardship?
5. How many times has my desire for righteousness cost me a job, a relationship, or my safety?
6. Lord, deepen my hunger and thirst for righteousness.
7. Lord, help me to receive you worthily, to crave you in the Sacrament of Holy Communion.

The Fifth Blessing

Blessed are the merciful, for they shall receive mercy.

1. What does the fifth blessing mean to me; what does it mean for the Church?
2. What does praying *"And forgive us our trespasses, as we forgive those who trespass against us"* teach me; what does it teach the Church about the fifth blessing?
3. How did Jacob's son Joseph model the fifth blessing?
4. How do I feel about the idea that God will show me mercy and forgive me in the same way that I show mercy to and forgive others?
5. Lord, deepen my dependence on you and increase my hunger for righteousness so that I might learn to forgive as you forgive me and show mercy as show mercy to me.
6. How often have I shown mercy and forgiveness to those closest to me, especially my wife, if I am married?
7. Lord, deepen my dependence on you and increase my hunger for righteousness so that I might learn to forgive my spouse to whom I am bound and blessed through the Sacrament of Holy Matrimony.

The Sixth Blessing

Blessed are the clean of heart, for they will see God.

1. What does the sixth blessing mean to me; what does it mean for the Church?
2. What does praying *"And lead us not into temptation"* teach me; what does it teach the Church about the sixth blessing?
3. How did Moses model the sixth blessing?
4. How many times and in how many ways has God surprised me with his presence?
5. How did I feel at those moments?
6. Has God prompted me to tell someone or do something after those moments?
7. Have I said and done those things?
8. When have I come closest to "Seeing God's Face?"
9. Lord, help me see you and respond better the next time you reveal yourself to me, even in my darkest hours, whether in bodily or spiritual suffering so that I might receive your healing grace through the Sacrament of the Anointing of the Sick.

The Seventh Blessing

Blessed are the peacemakers, for they shall be called children of God.

1. What does the seventh blessing mean to me; what does it mean for the Church?
2. What does praying *"But deliver us from evil"* teach me; what does it teach the Church about the seventh blessing?
3. How did David model the seventh blessing?
4. How often do I pray for those who oppose me or those who seek me harm?
5. How many times have I disrupted the peace in my home?
6. Has my family or any part of it become the enemy?
7. Lord, help me to release past injustices done to me and teach me to look for and repent of the injustices I have heaped on others.
8. Lord, teach me to honor and serve those whom you have called through the Sacrament of Holy Orders.

The Eighth Blessing

Blessed are they who are persecuted for the sake of righteousness, for theirs is the kingdom of heaven.

1. What does the eighth blessing mean to me; what does it mean for the Church?
2. What does the priest praying *"Deliver us, Lord, we pray, from every evil, graciously grant peace in our days, that, by the help of your mercy, we may be always free from sin and safe from all distress, as we await the blessed hope and the coming of our Savior, Jesus Christ"* during Mass teach me; what does it teach the Church about the eighth blessing?
3. How did John the Baptist model the eighth blessing?
4. Would I be willing to suffer for anyone, let alone my enemies?
5. Would I be willing to die for a person of another faith?
6. Would I be willing to die for a member of my family?
7. Will I speak, live, and die for Christ?
8. Lord, fill me with your presence. Teach me to live a Sacramental life.

The Ninth Blessing

Blessed are you when they insult you and persecute you and utter every kind of evil against you [falsely] because of me. Rejoice and be glad, for your reward will be great in heaven.

1. What does the ninth blessing mean to me; what does it mean for the Church?
2. Why did Christ teach the Church to pray, *"For thine is the kingdom, the power and the glory,"* after the priest prays the embolism?
3. How does the relationship of Jesus Christ and his Church model the ninth blessing?
4. How often do I rejoice in your presence during Mass, Lord?
5. How often do I rejoice in your presence when I am not in Mass?
6. Does my witness give others cause to rejoice?
7. Lord, fill me with lasting joy.
8. Teach and enable me to do your will completely, not partially, and always now, not later.
9. Teach me, Lord, to build a life that can withstand the rains/temptations, hardships/floods, and cares/winds of the world/this evil generation.
10. Please, Lord, help me see your face in the faces of my neighbors.

REFERENCES

Note: Except for the Lord's Prayer, which is given in the words said in Mass used by the United States Conference of Catholic Bishops (USCCB), all scripture quotes have been taken from the New American Bible Revised Edition ("NABRE"). https://bible.usccb.org/bible

www.ingramcontent.com/pod-product-compliance
Lightning Source LLC
Chambersburg PA
CBHW070100080526
44586CB00013B/1139